Daily Mind Builders™
Language Arts

Daily Mind Builders™ products available in print or eBook form.
Language Arts • Science • Social Studies

Written by
Jennifer Gottstein

Graphic Design by
Annette Langenstein

© 2009
THE CRITICAL THINKING CO.™
www.CriticalThinking.com
Phone: 800-458-4849 • Fax: 541-756-1758
1991 Sherman Ave., Suite 200 • North Bend • OR 97459
ISBN 978-1-60144-201-7

MIX
Paper from responsible sources
FSC® C011935

ABOUT THE AUTHOR

Jennifer Gottstein

Earlier in this century, when I began my teaching career, I went looking for that perfect activity that would start each school day off right. I had always loved activities that challenge the mind and thought these types of activities would be a good way to begin each school day. I soon discovered that higher level thinking activities are not as readily available as I had imagined. I then decided to find realistic situations that could be presented as a critical thinking activity. My first efforts in this direction were greeted by such enthusiasm that I soon realized I was onto something. My classes were asking for a new, realistic activity each day and were disappointed on the days when I failed to produce one.

From these early efforts, the three-book series of *Daily Mind Builders*™ was born. I would like to thank the students for their continuous enthusiasm, cooperation, and support in the writing of these three volumes. I also want to acknowledge the support given to me by my parents and friends for this project. They acted as unpaid, yet cheerful research assistants, who helped me assemble much of the raw material that went into these books. I am very grateful for their guidance and support.

TABLE OF CONTENTS

Introduction

The Value of These Activities

Each daily activity page includes two exercises. The first is a short story that requires careful reading and inferential reasoning to answer the question at the end. The second activity involves deductive thinking, and is designed to build vocabulary and stimulate associative thinking skills.

In addition to waking up sleepy brains for the day's lessons, these short, fun, daily activity pages develop the most important reading comprehension skill found on all standardized reading tests–synthesizing disparate information and using the result to produce a reasonable conclusion. Every *Daily Mind Builders™* exercise develops this key reading skill.

When to Use These Activities

Each *Daily Mind Builders™* is meant to be a short 5-10 minute activity, and can be a great way to start a lesson. However, there is no bad time to teach critical thinking and the *Daily Mind Builders™* can be inserted whenever time permits at any time during the school day, e.g.:

1. Motivational beginning activity used as an addition to the curriculum.
2. Culminating activity after a lesson or at the end of the day.
3. Fill-in activity when there is an awkward time break during the school day.
4. A valid educational activity for students who finish assigned activities earlier than their classmates.

The best use of this book is when presented as a non-threatening, non-graded, fun activity where students are praised for all logical answers even if they don't happen to be the correct answers. In critical thinking, the journey is as important as the destination, and all reasonable efforts at critical thinking should be commended.

Teaching Suggestions

Most of the stories in the first activity are based on historical events, with a few exceptions (myths/legends). The answer in the back of the book is the ideal conclusion one would expect to reach. Sentence evidence answers are based on this conclusion.

Optional Thinking Map

Some students benefit by filling out the optional *Daily Mind Builders™* Thinking Map (vi). On page vii is an example of a completed thinking map.

What is Critical Thinking?

Critical thinking is the identification and evaluation of evidence to guide decision making. A critical thinker uses broad, in-depth analysis of evidence to make decisions and to communicate his/her beliefs clearly and accurately.

It's All About Evidence

As a critical thinker, you need to identify and evaluate evidence to make and support your conclusions. Evidence can also prove your conclusion is correct. To help you understand what evidence is, read the six sentences below and try to find the evidence that tells you...

Who Helped Themselves to Peanut Butter and Jam?

[1]Eddie's mom looked at Eddie and his baby sister, Sarah. [2]There were crumbs on the floor, and Sarah had peanut butter and jam on her chin. [3]"Did you two help yourselves to the peanut butter and jam without asking?" asked Eddie's mom. [4]Eddie pointed to Sarah and said, "I didn't but Sarah did." [5]He quickly grabbed a clean paper towel and handed it to his mother so she could wipe Sarah's chin. [6]As he handed the towel to his mother, she saw peanut butter and jam on Eddie's fingers.

Information in sentence 2 tells us that that "Sarah had peanut butter and jam on her chin." We know from this evidence that she was into the peanut butter and jam. Sentence 6 tells us that Eddie had peanut butter and jam on his fingers. We know from this evidence that Eddie could be lying to his mother. The evidence in sentences 2 and 6 supports the conclusion that both Eddie and Sarah were into the peanut butter and jam.

The first activity on each page asks you to identify the best evidence for your conclusion. To help you identify a particular sentence, all of the sentences in the story are numbered. When looking for the best evidence for your conclusion, be sure to reread the story carefully.

Daily Mind Builders™ **Thinking Map (Optional)**

Question: _____

_____

⬇

Who?	
Did What?	
Where?	
When?	
Why?	

⬇

Conclusion:

⬇

Evidence for Conclusion:

Daily Mind Builders™ **Thinking Map Example**

Question: <u>What is the name of C.L. Grigg's soft drink?</u>

<u> </u>

Who?	
	C.L. Grigg
Did What?	
	Invented a soft drink and kept the creation of the name a secret.
Where?	
	Unknown
When?	
	1929
Why?	
	The name of the soft drink relates to throwing dice, the pastime he was playing.

Conclusion:
C.L. Grigg invented the soft drink 7 Up.

Evidence for Conclusion:
Most popular theory is that he came up with the name while playing one of his favorite pastimes of throwing dice.

GAMBLING ON THE NAME OF A SODA?

*Read the true story below, then make an inference
based on the evidence in the story.*

[1]C. L. Grigg invented a soft drink in 1929 that is still enjoyed today. [2]As far as anyone knows, Mr. Grigg never revealed how he came up with the name for his soft drink. [3]Because of this secrecy many theories have sprung up over the years to explain the name. [4]One of the most popular theories is that C.L. Grigg came up with the name while engaging in his favorite pastime of throwing dice. [5]What is the name of C. L. Grigg's soft drink?

Your conclusion: _____

Which sentence has the best evidence to support your conclusion? _____

WORD CONNECTIONS

fling	down	nag	arms	master
mess	duck	hard	line	join

*Write the word from the choice box that best matches the
meaning of both word sets.   Use each choice box word once.*

1. weapons   limbs   _____

2. feathers   dejected   _____

3. waterfowl   avoid   _____

4. throw   wild time   _____

5. difficult   solid   _____

6. connect   accompany   _____

7. boundary   cord   _____

8. chief   control   _____

9. hodgepodge   meddle   _____

10. old horse   scold   _____

WHAT WAS THE STICKY INVENTION?

Read the true story below, then make an inference
based on the evidence in the story.

[1]Way back in the 1940s, a Swiss inventor by the name of George de Mestral took his dog for a walk. [2]Nothing unusual in this as he took his beloved dog for a walk every day. [3]But this time, upon returning home, George discovered that his dog had gotten into a cocklebur patch and his dog was covered with cockleburs. [4]George then spent the next hour patiently picking burrs out of his dog's fur. [5]If you have ever tried to pick burrs out of fur you would know what a difficult job this is as the burrs don't want to let go. [6]This incident gave George a brilliant idea for a new invention that is widely used today. [7]What did he invent?

Your conclusion: _____

Which sentence has the best evidence to support your conclusion? _____

SPEAKING JAPANESE

butter	T-shirt	speed	chocolate	raincoat	toilet paper
	jacket	speed	teacher	cigarettes	ballpoint

Write the English words from the choice box that best match
the Japanese words below. Some Japanese words are
spelled incorrectly to make them easier to pronounce.

1. tabako   _____

2. supido   _____

3. boropen   _____

4. tishatsu   _____

5. sensei   _____

6. toiretto pepa _____

7. reinkoto   _____

8. jaketto   _____

9. bata   _____

10. chokoreto _____

AT LAST, JEFFERSON DAVIS WAS BORN!

Read the true story below, then make an inference
based on the evidence in the story.

[1]Jefferson F. Davis was a famous American who held various political offices and served as president of the Confederate States of America during the Civil War. [2]He was born in 1808 and was the youngest of 10 children. [3]In 1808, medical science was not nearly as advanced as it is today. [4]His birth was considered something of a medical miracle at the time because his mother was the very advanced age of 47 when he was born. [5]His parents were logical people with a sense of humor. [6]What does the initial "F" stand for in his name?

Your conclusion: _____

Which sentences have the best evidence to support your conclusion? _____ _____

WHAT'S THE RELATIONSHIP?

The words in the shaded box have a logical connection to each
other. Circle the word below the shaded box that shares the
relationship. Then explain the relationship between the words.

1. May I count on you?

tool	formidable	sixpence	atelier

       commode   loathe   tension

Why?_____

2. Don't be a royal pain in the neck.

queensize	discount	breaking	pearl

       dukedom   marriage   elusion

Why?_____

3. Don't let this drive you crazy.

afford	dodger	geometry	saturnine

       spigot   recite   plexus

Why?_____

WHAT WAS VON BAYER'S GIRLFRIEND'S NAME?

*Read the true story below, then make an inference
based on the evidence in the story.*

[1]Adolph Von Bayer is most famous for discovering aspirin in the 19th century and founding the drug company that is still making aspirin today. [2]But Von Bayer didn't stop at making aspirin as he also was the first person who was able to synthesize barbiturates. [3]Barbiturates are a group of drugs that are used to calm people down or make them sleepy. [4]At the same time Von Bayer was creating barbiturates he fell in love and was dating a very attractive woman. [5]What was his girlfriend's first name?

Your conclusion: _____

Which sentence has the best evidence to support your conclusion? _____

RHYME TIME

pact	ducky	fat	fickle	beagle	mice	mirth
dune	fuse	nice	cat	pickle	trip	birth
lucky	muse	intact	legal	ship	tune	

*Write two rhyming words from the choice box to create a definition
for each item below. Use each choice box word once.*

1. polite rodents   _____   _____

2. stout feline   _____   _____

3. ocean voyage   _____   _____

4. fortunate waterfowl   _____   _____

5. lawful hound   _____   _____

6. disloyal cucumber   _____   _____

7. unbroken treaty   _____   _____

8. electrical poet   _____   _____

9. born laughing   _____   _____

10. desert song   _____   _____

NAME THIS FAST FOOD

Read the true story below, then make an inference
based on the evidence in the story.

[1]In 1946, World War II was just over and Glen Bell was discharged from the Marines and looking for something to do with his life. [2]He decided the town of San Bernardino, California, could support another hot dog stand and went into the business of selling hot dogs. [3]By 1952, Glen was running three food stands and had expanded his menu to include chili dogs and hamburgers. [4]It was then that Glen Bell had the idea of adding another item to his menu that he sold for 19 cents and became very popular. [5]In the course of time it made Glen a very wealthy man. [6]What was that food item?

Your conclusion: _____

Which sentence has the best evidence to support your conclusion? _____

SPEAKING ITALIAN

water	library	campground	ghosts	grow plants	team
	train	short time	teenagers	toothpaste	

Write the English words from the choice box that best
match the Italian words below. Some Italian words are
spelled incorrectly to make them easier to pronounce.

1. spiriti _____

2. squadra _____

3. treno _____

4. acqua _____

5. adolescenti _____

6. biblioteca _____

7. breve _____

8. campeggio _____

9. coltivare _____

10. dentifricio _____

LINCOLN AND KENNEDY SHARE WHAT VISIT?

*Read the true story below, then make an inference
based on the evidence in the story.*

[1]There are many odd connections between the assassinations of President Lincoln and President Kennedy. [2]For instance, Kennedy was elected to the House of Representatives in 1946, and Lincoln was elected to the House in 1846. [3]And, both presidents were succeeded in office by vice-presidents named Johnson. [4]Also, Lincoln was shot in Ford's Theater and Kennedy was shot in a car made by the Ford Motor Company. [5]It was rumored that President Kennedy visited the famous actress Marilyn Monroe shortly before she died. [6]Shortly, before he was assassinated, what city and state did President Lincoln visit?

Your conclusion: _____

Which sentences have the best evidence to support your conclusion? _____   _____

FIGURE OUT THE ORDER

*The story below contains events that happened in order. One thing happened
first, another second, and so on. Below the story is a chart that lists all the
possibilities for each event. Using the clues provided in the story allows you to
cross out possibilities under each number until you know the correct order.*

HOT POTATO

George, Gail, Ginny, and Greg were going on a double date and walking down the street. The taller of the two girls saw a potato on the sidewalk and picked it up only to discover it was very hot. She flipped it in the air where it was caught by the tallest person in the group. The tallest person then flipped it in the air where it was caught by a close relative. That person then flipped it in the air where it was finally dropped back on the sidewalk. Gail and Ginny aren't related to anyone in the story. Ginny is taller than Gail. Greg is the shortest child in his family.

FIRST	SECOND	THIRD	FOURTH
George	George	George	George
Gail	Gail	Gail	Gail
Ginny	Ginny	Ginny	Ginny
Greg	Greg	Greg	Greg

1st _____   2nd _____   3rd _____   4th _____

POINTING THE WAY

*Read the true story below, then make an inference
based on the evidence in the story.*

[1]There is a plant common to the middle part of the United States that gets its name from the way it behaves. [2]This plant points its lower leaves in a north and south direction. [3]By doing so, these leaves avoid the harsh midday sun but get the milder full early morning and late afternoon sunlight. [4]What is the common name of this clever plant that knows how to point its leaves the right way?

Your conclusion: _____

Which sentence has the best evidence to support your conclusion? _____

SPEAKING RUSSIAN

sauce	milk	lightbulb	automobile	backbone
pig	chocolate	lemonade	fruit	diabetic

*Write the English words from the choice box that best
match the Russian words below. Some Russian words are
spelled incorrectly to make them easier to pronounce.*

1. mashinu _____

2. diabyet _____

3. spina _____

4. soous _____

5. froukty _____

6. limonat _____

7. svininy _____

8. malako _____

9. shakalada _____

10. lampachka _____

WE'RE MRS. HANDLER'S KIDS

*Read the true story below, then make an inference
based on the evidence in the story.*

[1]Mrs. Ruth Handler was looking for ways to make some extra money. [2]In 1959, she had an idea for a new type of toy. [3]Mrs. Handler unveiled her new toy at the American Toy Fair held in New York City. [4]Her toy is still very popular to this day. [5]Mrs. Handler was the mother of two children. [6]She had one girl and one boy. [7]What were their first names?

Your conclusion: _____

Which sentences have the best evidence to support your conclusion? _____ _____

WHAT'S THE RELATIONSHIP?

*The words in the shaded box have a logical connection to each
other. Circle the word below the shaded box that shares the
relationship. Then explain the relationship between the words.*

1. All living things have a beginning. And an ending.

acid	December	roam	may

yellow   sliding   misfit

Why? _____

2. Napoleon said, "Able was I ere I saw Elba."

madam	radar	gag	noon

cluck   chirp   peep

Why? _____

3. Now I know my ABCs…

unction	under	unenlightened	unforgettable

unlikable   unmarried   ungrateful

Why? _____

LET ME WRAP THAT UP FOR YOU

Read the true story below, then make an inference
based on the evidence in the story.

[1]Many inventors have given credit to their wives for providing the inspiration for their inventions. [2]In 1920, Earle Dickson gave the credit for his invention to his wife, Josephine. [3]She was by all accounts a wonderful wife but she did have one failing. [4]Josephine was very clumsy in the kitchen and was always burning and cutting herself by accident. [5]What did Earle Dickson invent?

Your conclusion: _____

Which sentence has the best evidence to support your conclusion? _____

RHYME TIME

froggy	Bill's	toil	grin	letter	mouse	togs
soil	louse	brain	course	pills	horse	beet
twin	dog's	groggy	sweet	getter	pain	

Write two rhyming words from the choice box to create a definition
for each item below. Use each choice box word once.

1. farm labor   _____   _____

2. computer hacker   _____   _____

3. sugar producer   _____   _____

4. received mail   _____   _____

5. double smile   _____   _____

6. pet's clothes   _____   _____

7. hurting head   _____   _____

8. William's medicine _____   _____

9. dizzy amphibian   _____   _____

10. feedbag of oats   _____   _____

WHAT IS THE ENGLISH WORD FOR THAT MOUNTAIN?

*Read the true story below, then make an inference
based on the evidence in the story.*

[1]In ancient times, the only way to wash clothes was to go down to the local river. [2]In Italy, the ancient Romans had one particular small mountain they used to sacrifice animals to their Roman gods. [3]Their method of sacrifice was to kill and burn different kinds of animals. [4]This created lots of animal fat and ashes, which formed a natural detergent when combined together. [5]Women discovered that clothes washed in the part of the river where the fat and ashes drained came out cleaner than clothes washed in other parts of the river. [6]What is the English word that came from the Italian name for that mountain?

Your conclusion: _____

Which sentences have the best evidence to support your conclusion? _____ _____

SPEAKING FRENCH

United States	bank	OK	rearview mirror	exit
I'm sorry	coins	holidays	hour	round trip

*Write the English words from the choice box that best
match the French words below. Some French words are
spelled incorrectly to make them easier to pronounce.*

1. desole _____

2. d'accord _____

3. Etats-Unis _____

4. banque _____

5. pieces _____

6. heure _____

7. aller-retour _____

8. vacances _____

9. sortie _____

10. retroviseur _____

CAN YOU GUESS THE NAMES?

*Read the true story below, then make an inference
based on the evidence in the story.*

[1]Glenn Seaborg was a famous scientist who did his work at his beloved University of California in Berkeley, California. [2]He discovered 10 different atomic elements. [3]The one who discovers a new element gets the honor of naming it and Glenn Seaborg gave the elements names such as Americium, Curium, Einsteinium, Fermium, Mendelevium, and Nobelium. [4]He never named an element after himself although another scientist who discovered an atomic element named it Seaborgium in his honor. [5]In 1950, Seaborg discovered and named two more atomic elements. [6]Can you guess what he named them?

Your conclusion: _____

Which sentences have the best evidence to support your conclusion? _____ _____

RHYME IT

mopped	dance	slash	teach	glare	bake
	clap	dried	trees	grow	

*Write one rhyming word from the choice box to create a
definition for each item below. Use each choice box word once.*

1. reach the children   _____

2. make cookies   _____

3. stare in anger   _____

4. fried with a hairdryer   _____

5. slopped the floor clean   _____

6. these give shade   _____

7. gash with a knife   _____

8. sow the seeds   _____

9. slap your hands   _____

10. prance to a tune   _____

SO WHAT WAS SOUSA'S FIRST LAST NAME?

Read the true story below, then make an inference
based on the evidence in the story.

[1]John Phillip Sousa was a famous composer and bandleader in the United States of America. [2]He wrote many marches such as "Stars and Stripes Forever" and the "Washington Post March" that are still played today on patriotic occasions. [3]Some published accounts say that he so loved the United States of America that he changed his last name to demonstrate his devotion to this country. [4]What was Sousa's last name before he changed it to show his love for this country?

Your conclusion: _____

Which sentence has the best evidence to support your conclusion? _____

WHAT'S THE RELATIONSHIP?

The words in the shaded box have a logical connection to each
other. Circle the word below the shaded box that shares the
relationship. Then explain the relationship between the words.

1. You'll fly through this one.

scowl	tomahawks	scarecrow	graven

spider   gullible   plantation

Why? _____

2. Oh, fur goodness sake!

share	ratio	usable	molecule

spacious   determine   elephant

Why? _____

3. This may be two easy.

bookstall	deeprooted	sleepless	shatterproof

shellfish   toothbrush   football

Why? _____

ON WHAT RIVER IS CAMBRIDGE LOCATED?

Read the true story below, then make an inference
based on the evidence in the story.

[1]Cambridge University in Great Britain was founded way back in 1209, when some scholars left Oxford University to start their own institution of higher learning. [2]Cambridge University is located in the town of Cambridge which was a favorable location because it is only about 50 miles north of London and had a steady supply of water used for both drinking and transportation. [3]On what river is Cambridge located?

Your conclusion: _____

Which sentence has the best evidence to support your conclusion? _____

SPEAKING ENGLISH

drawer	training wheels	office gossip	farmer	garbage can
oven timer	toilet tissue	bobby pins	back scrubber	bar of soap

Write the American words from the choice box that
best match the traditional English words below.

1. griff   _____

2. grainer   _____

3. stabilizers   _____

4. hair grips   _____

5. dust bin   _____

6. sliding box   _____

7. flesh brush   _____

8. loo paper   _____

9. wash ball   _____

10. pinger   _____

NOTE: The traditional English words for the activity "Speaking English" were taken from *Hippocrene Language and Travel Guide to Britain.*

WHAT IS THIS FISHY NAME?

*Read the true story below, then make an inference
based on the evidence in the story.*

[1]Early Indians all along the west coast of North America used to catch an 8-inch-long saltwater fish when the fish traveled up rivers to spawn. [2]This tasty fish was so oily that the Indians discovered they could dry them and set them afire when they needed a light at night. [3]Pioneers saw how the Indians used the fish and gave it a logical name. [4]What is the name of this fish?

Your conclusion: _____

Which sentence has the best evidence to support your conclusion? _____

RHYME TIME

limber	sub	dingo	dress	towel	tramp	doom
vest	grub	lingo	fowl	trial	gloom	haze	press
	damp	file	best	timber	blaze		

*Write two rhyming words from the choice box to create a definition
for each item below. Use each choice box word once.*

1. Australian dog talk _____ _____

2. underwater food _____ _____

3. fear of death _____ _____

4. newspaper clothing _____ _____

5. smoky campfire _____ _____

6. flexible wood _____ _____

7. finest waistcoat _____ _____

8. turkey bath cloth _____ _____

9. a wet hobo _____ _____

10. court records _____ _____

CAN YOU NAME THE CREATION?

Read the true story below, then make an inference
based on the evidence in the story.

[1]About a century ago, the country of Macedonia was famous for the large variety of ethnic peoples that lived there. [2]Macedonia was the home of Turks, Serbs, Pomaks, Roumanians, Vlachs, Greeks, Albanians, and Arnauts. [3]A French chef created a dish he named in honor of Macedonia. [4]Can you guess the type of dish it was?

Your conclusion: _____

Which sentences have the best evidence to support your conclusion? _____   _____

FIGURE OUT THE ORDER

The story below contains events that happened in order. One
thing happened first, another second, and so on. Below the story
is a chart that lists all the possibilities for each event. Using the
clues provided in the story allows you to cross out possibilities
under each number until you know the correct order.

RUN FOR YOUR LIFE!

Four mice were running to get away from the farmer's wife who was chasing them with a large knife and blood in her eye. Their names were Minnie, Mickey, Mopey, and Felix. All of them escaped serious injury although one mouse needed stitches and a bandage. Minnie was faster than two other mice but wasn't the fastest mouse. Felix was scratched in the back by the panicked mouse running behind him. Mickey received no injuries from the mouse running immediately behind him. Felix is a slower runner than Minnie. In what order did the mice escape from the crazed farmer's wife?

FIRST	SECOND	THIRD	FOURTH
Minnie	Minnie	Minnie	Minnie
Mickey	Mickey	Mickey	Mickey
Mopey	Mopey	Mopey	Mopey
Felix	Felix	Felix	Felix

1st _____   2nd _____   3rd _____   4th _____

WHAT WAS SO UNUSUAL ABOUT THE EXHIBIT?

*Read the true story below, then make an inference
based on the evidence in the story.*

[1]Henri Matisse, who died in 1954, was a French artist and one of the most important painters of the 20th century. [2]Some of his paintings made no attempt to create the illusion of reality but relied on color and lines to produce patterns and a sense of movement. [3]One of Matisse's masterpieces was entitled "Le Bateau" and was exhibited at the Museum of Modern Art in 1961 to great public and critical acclaim. [4]This masterpiece was exhibited for 47 days in an unusual fashion. [5]What was so unusual about the way "Le Bateau" was exhibited?

Your conclusion: _____

Which sentences have the best evidence to support your conclusion? _____ _____

SPEAKING ITALIAN

dolphin	law	English	coffee	raincoat	kind
	telephone	to enter	city	accident	

*Write the English words from the choice box that best
match the Italian words below. Some Italian words are
spelled incorrectly to make them easier to pronounce.*

1. caffe   _____

2. telefonino   _____

3. citta   _____

4. delfino   _____

5. entrare   _____

6. gentile   _____

7. legge   _____

8. incidente   _____

9. impermeabile   _____

10. Inglese   _____

WHY THE TOM THUMB GOLF COURSE?

*Read the true story below, then make an inference
based on the evidence in the story.*

[1]Tom Thumb was a famous circus performer who was considered one of the smallest adult human beings on earth during his lifetime. [2]In 1929, John Carter built his first golf course in Chattanooga, Tennessee. [3]Carter named his golf course the "Tom Thumb Golf Course." [4]Can you guess why he gave it this name?

Your conclusion: _____

Which sentences have the best evidence to support your conclusion? _____ _____

WHAT'S THE RELATIONSHIP?

The words in the shaded box have a logical connection to each other. Circle the word below the shaded box that shares the relationship. Then explain the relationship between the words.

1. "Pat, I think I'll buy a vowel."

splat	trend	grill	trophy

weedy   beard   spun

Why? _____

2. I triple-dog-dare you to get this one right.

almanac	bubble	catechetical	dreaded

bloodless   effete   egoistic

Why? _____

3. This one will hit you sooner or later.

baseball	golf ball	tennis ball	Ping-Pong ball

basketball   softball   football

Why? _____

CAN YOU GUESS THE HORSE'S NAME?

*Read the true story below, then make an inference
based on the evidence in the story.*

[1]Many people believe that the greatest racehorse of all time was Man O'War. [2]This horse was so fast that nobody ever thought he would lose a race. [3]Mostly, this thinking proved to be true as Man O'War won every race he ever ran except one. [4]On August 13, 1919, Man O'War lost for the one and only time in his legendary career. [5]People were astonished by two things concerning this event. [6]The first, of course, was that this overwhelming favorite could be defeated. [7]The second was the name of the only horse ever to defeat the seemingly invincible Man O'War. [8]The name of this horse perfectly described the outcome of the race. [9]Can you guess the name of this horse?

Your conclusion: _____

Which sentence has the best evidence to support your conclusion? _____

WORD CONNECTIONS

cross	hand	fork	fire	general	cold
contract	fall	form	fair		

*Write the word from the choice box that best matches the
meaning of both word sets.   Use each choice box word once.*

1. clock pointer   body part   _____

2. widespread   army leader   _____

3. shape   printed document   _____

4. eating tool   division   _____

5. combustion   discarge from a job   _____

6. autumn   descend quickly   _____

7. just   festival   _____

8. pass over   cranky   _____

9. legal agreement   shrink   _____

10. frigid   viral infection   _____

WHAT DID THE FOOTBALL TEAM DO?

*Read the true story below, then make an inference
based on the evidence in the story. .*

[1]Gallaudet College is a school for deaf students. [2]Deaf students often communicate through the use of sign language. [3]This means it is difficult to have a private conversation as everyone who can read sign language can read what you are saying if they can see you talking with your hands. [4]In the 1890s, the Gallaudet football team was in trouble because the opposing teams were reading their hand signals and knew what play was coming next. [5]To solve this problem the Gallaudet team was the first to start doing something that all football teams have been doing ever since. [6]What did the team do?

Your conclusion: _____

Which sentences have the best evidence to support your conclusion? _____ _____

SPEAKING GERMAN

to drink	below	father	aunt	milk	to steal
	sun	telescope	above	price	

*Write the English words from the choice box that best
match the German words below. Some German words are
spelled incorrectly to make them easier to pronounce.*

1. stehlen   _____

2. vater   _____

3. unter   _____

4. preis   _____

5. sonne   _____

6. tante   _____

7. teleskop   _____

8. trinken   _____

9. uber   _____

10. milch   _____

WHAT ONE TEAM WAS FORMED FROM TWO?

*Read the true story below, then make an inference
based on the evidence in the story.*

[1]The year was 1943, World War II was raging, and most of our young men were in uniform. [2]This made it difficult for professional sports teams to get enough players to field a respectable team. [3]In the National Football League, things got so bad that the Pittsburgh Steelers and the Philadelphia Eagles decided to combine their players into one team. [4]What was the name of this team?

Your conclusion: _____

Which sentence has the best evidence to support your conclusion? _____

FIGURE OUT THE ORDER

*The story below contains events that happened in order. One
thing happened first, another second, and so on. Below the story
is a chart that lists all the possibilities for each event. Using the
clues provided in the story allows you to cross out possibilities
under each number until you know the correct order.*

ICE CREAM WAITERS?

Four children named Wilbur, William, Walter, and Wallace were waiting in line at the ice cream store. The child served first ordered one scoop of vanilla ice cream served on a cone. The child served second ordered a chocolate sundae. The third in line ordered a strawberry milk shake. The fourth in line ordered one scoop of vanilla and one scoop of strawberry ice cream served in the same cone. Wallace was allergic to strawberries and ate his ice cream by licking it. Walter ordered after William but wasn't last in line. Now figure out the order in which all four children were served.

FIRST	SECOND	THIRD	FOURTH
Wilbur	Wilbur	Wilbur	Wilbur
William	William	William	William
Walter	Walter	Walter	Walter
Wallace	Wallace	Wallace	Wallace

1st _____   2nd _____   3rd _____   4th _____

CAN YOU GUESS THE TITLE?

*Read the true story below, then make an inference
based on the evidence in the story.*

[1]When Wade Boggs was playing 3rd base for the Boston Red Sox, he was famous for his efforts in chasing after foul-tipped balls and catching them for an out. [2]Another of his claims to fame was his love of chicken and he claimed to eat it at least once a day. [3]In 1984, Wade and his wife co-wrote a chicken cookbook that included many clever ideas on different ways to prepare chicken. [4]They came up with the title for their cookbook by playing with words associated with Wade's baseball fame and, of course, cooking birds such as chickens. [5]Can you guess the title of their cookbook?

Your conclusion: _____

Which sentences have the best evidence to support your conclusion? _____   _____

WORD CONNECTIONS

trip	produce		press	pack	use
utter	tank		toll	pass	second

*Write the word from the choice box that best matches the
meaning of both word sets.   Use each choice box word once.*

1. bundle   load   _____

2. decline   proceed   _____

3. vegetables   create   _____

4. time measure   support   _____

5. container   weapon   _____

6. speak   absolute   _____

7. apply   purpose   _____

8. journey   stumble   _____

9. tax   ring   _____

10. squeeze   newspapers   _____

WHISTLE TO SAVE LIVES

*Read the true story below, then make an inference
based on the evidence in the story.*

[1]In the early days of railroads, it became vitally important to warn people that a train was approaching. [2]It is still important today and trains now use a very loud air horn to warn people that a train is approaching. [3]But in the early days of railroading there was no good way to warn people until someone finally invented a train whistle that was loud enough to be heard from a long distance away. [4]Who invented the train whistle that is credited with saving many lives?

Your conclusion: _____

Which sentence has the best evidence to support your conclusion? _____

SPEAKING JAPANESE

lamp	golf	lunch	cheese	helmet	concert
restaurant	soccer	laundromat	football		

*Write the English words from the choice box that best match
the Japanese words below. Some Japanese words are
spelled incorrectly to make them easier to pronounce.*

1. chizu _____

2. koin randori _____

3. futto boru _____

4. sakka _____

5. ranchi _____

6. gorufu _____

7. konsato _____

8. resutoran _____

9. rampu _____

10. herumetto _____

WHAT INSTRUMENT CAUGHT THAT BALL?

*Read the true story below, then make an inference
based on the evidence in the story.*

[1]At the 1965 All Star baseball game, the great Willie Stargell of the Pittsburgh Pirates hit a towering home run over the fence and into the ranks of a marching band that was waiting to perform after the game. [2]The band member who caught the baseball was said to have an unfair advantage over everyone else in the band. [3]What instrument did that band member play?

Your conclusion: _____

Which sentence has the best evidence to support your conclusion? _____

WHAT'S THE RELATIONSHIP?

*The words in the shaded box have a logical connection to each
other. Circle the word below the shaded box that shares the
relationship. Then explain the relationship between the words.*

1. Don't go out on a limb.

supine	croak	fireman	helm

pancake   palmistry   forehead

Why? _____

2. It took me days to make up my mind.

monster	wedding	sunder	satisfy

fritter   belch   sibilant

Why? _____

3. Work on this independently.

pencil	depend	pendant	open

panic   suspense   pendulum

Why? _____

WHAT'S A COMBAT EMPLACEMENT EVACUATOR?

Read the true story below, then make an inference
based on the evidence in the story.

[1]For reasons of its own, the military likes to give oddly detailed names to the most common objects that it uses. [2]For instance, the military issues its soldiers something called a "combat emplacement evacuator." [3]It might help you to know what combat soldiers use as emplacements but what would us non-soldiers call this "combat emplacement evacuator?"

Your conclusion: _____

Which sentence has the best evidence to support your conclusion? _____

RHYME TIME

slumber	money	bird	loaned	slime	flat	lumber	ship
tool	bone	drip	funny	phone	curd	prime	
jewel	goo	cat	shoe	crone			

Write the two rhyming words from the choice box to create a
definition for each item below. Use each choice box word once.

1. fake dollar   _____   _____

2. call witch   _____   _____

3. borrowed tibia   _____   _____

4. diamond cutter   _____   _____

5. boat leak   _____   _____

6. parrot cheese   _____   _____

7. best scum   _____   _____

8. road-killed tabby   _____   _____

9. wood sleep   _____   _____

10. footgear gum   _____   _____

WHAT NAME DID HISTORY GIVE TO THIS BATTLE?

*Read the true story below, then make an inference
based on the evidence in the story.*

¹The year was 1838 and tensions were running oven-temperature high between the countries of France and Mexico. ²Tart words were exchanged and events reached a boiling point in Mexico City when Mexican soldiers attacked a French bakery, known for its fine éclairs and cream puffs, and destroyed it. ³This incident briefly gave rise to a war between the two countries before cooler heads prevailed and relations returned to a more normal sweet roll of diplomatic relations. ⁴What name did history give to this little known war?

Your conclusion: _____

Which sentence has the best evidence to support your conclusion? _____

FIGURE OUT THE ORDER

The story below contains events that happened in order. One thing happened first, another second, and so on. Below the story is a chart that lists all the possibilities for each event. Using the clues provided in the allows you to cross out possibilities under each number until you know the correct order.

THE BAG RACE

The four finalists in the bag race at a company picnic were, in no particular order, Don, Marie, Rikki, and Jerry. Don and Jerry were men and, oddly enough, Marie and Rikki were women. A woman finished last and Don didn't win the race but he did finish in front of Jerry and Rikki. Place the four finalists in the order in which they finished the race.

FIRST	SECOND	THIRD	FOURTH
Don	Don	Don	Don
Marie	Marie	Marie	Marie
Rikk	Rikki	Rikki	Rikki
Jerry	Jerry	Jerry	Jerry

1st _____ 2nd _____ 3rd _____ 4th _____

BERMAN SUED FOR WHAT?

*Read the true story below, then make an inference
based on the evidence in the story.*

[1]Reuben Berman loved going to baseball games. [2]But one thing Mr. Berman wanted to do at baseball games he wasn't allowed to do. [3]This bothered him so much that in 1927, he sued the New York Giants baseball team for the right to do the one thing at a baseball game that he wasn't allowed to do. [4]He won his lawsuit and since then many thousands of baseball fans have been able to do what Reuben Berman wanted to do way back in 1927. [5]What was Reuben Berman's lawsuit all about?

Your conclusion: _____

Which sentence has the best evidence to support your conclusion? _____

SPEAKING ITALIAN

to act	fast	stomach	vacation	public	addiction
	drugstore	luck	land	dictionary	

*Write the English words from the choice box that best
match the Italian words below. Some Italian words are
spelled incorrectly to make them easier to pronounce.*

1. dependenza _____

2. espresso _____

3. farmacia _____

4. fortuna _____

5. stomaco _____

6. terra _____

7. vacanze _____

8. vocabolario _____

9. recitare _____

10. pubblico _____

AN INDECENT CHICKEN?

*Read the true story below, then make an inference
based on the evidence in the story.*

[1]One of the major costs of processing chicken for sale is the expense of removing the feathers before the chickens can make it to our dinner plate. [2]Most people prefer eating their chicken without having to pick feathers out of their teeth. [3]Scientists set to work and in 1975, they came up with a featherless chicken. [4]But this new type of naked chicken never caught on with chicken growers because they soon were presented with another problem that added to their costs. [5]Can you deduce what the new problem was?

Your conclusion: _____

Which sentence has the best evidence to support your conclusion? _____

DEFINITIONS

wept	dock	pig	chew	read
jump	feed	raced	rat	ice

Write the word from the choice box that is described in the definition.

1. big hog _____

2. nice for skating _____

3. haste makes waste _____

4. a pier made of rock _____

5. chased by a cat _____

6. lead to dinner _____

7. kept crying _____

8. feed the mind _____

9. hopped the hump _____

10. turn food into goo _____

WHAT WAS GRINNELL'S MIDDLE NAME?

*Read the true story below, then make an inference
based on the evidence in the story.*

[1]John James Audubon became rich and famous in the 19th century by studying and painting the birds of North America. [2]His lifelike paintings and drawings are still sought after to this day. [3]His name became so associated with wildlife that the National Audubon Society, dedicated to conserving America's wildlife, was named in his honor. [4]This organization was founded in 1905 by a perfectly named George B. Grinnell. [5]What does his middle initial stand for?

Your conclusion: _____

Which sentence has the best evidence to support your conclusion? _____

SPEAKING FRENCH

sink	blanket	Chinese	campsite	women	bugs
	name	elevator	token	vacancy	

*Write the English words from the choice box that best
match the French words below. Some French words are
spelled incorrectly to make them easier to pronounce.*

1. dames _____

2. chambre libre _____

3. ascenseur _____

4. appelle _____

5. couverture _____

6. insectes _____

7. lavabo _____

8. emplacement _____

9. jeton _____

10. Chinois _____

WHAT'S THE MAGICAL WORD?

*Read the true story below, then make an inference
based on the evidence in the story.*

[1]There is a word, invented by the writers of the Captain Marvel comic books, that has come into general usage. [2]This magical word is associated with Solomon's wisdom, Hercules' strength, Atlas' stamina, Zeus' power, Achilles' courage, and Mercury's speed. [3]What is this word?

Your conclusion: _____

Which sentence has the best evidence to support your conclusion? _____

WHAT'S THE RELATIONSHIP?

The words in the shaded box have a logical connection to each other. Circle the word below the shaded box that shares the relationship. Then explain the relationship between the words.

1. Keep it clean.

soap flake	soapberry	soapiness	soap opera

soapsuds   soapbox   soapstones

Why?_____

2. There is no accounting for this puzzle.

mete	meteor	meteoric	metempirical

meteorograph   meteorologic   meteorological

Why? _____

3. This may be double the fun.

bookstall	weediness	woodcutter	seedless

poolroom   boondoggle   poppy seed

Why? _____

WHAT'S THE COMMON TIE WITH THESE NAMES?

*Read the true story below, then make an inference
based on the evidence in the story.*

[1]It may take awhile for it to come to you, but if you display intellectual fortitude and keep working at it, good fortune will be forthcoming. [2]The states of Alabama, Alaska, Hawaii, Indiana, Iowa, Kansas, Mississippi, Tennessee, and Utah all share the same thing in common when it comes to the spelling of their names. [3]What is it?

Your conclusion: _____

Which sentences have the best evidence to support your conclusion? _____   _____

SPEAKING ENGLISH

| ears | wonderful | flashlight | matches | preacher |
| pantry | clumsy | sausages | spendthrift | lazy person |

*Write the American words from the choice box that
best match the traditional English words below.*

1. lucifer   _____

2. torch   _____

3. larder   _____

4. devil dodger   _____

5. ham-fisted   _____

6. tabs   _____

7. squanderboats   _____

8. lead slinger   _____

9. spiffing   _____

10. snorkers   _____

WHICH HOLIDAY IS WHICH?

*Read the true story below, then make an inference
based on the evidence in the story.*

[1]One holiday of the year causes Americans to make the most phone calls as people reach out to make contact with somebody important. [2]Another holiday of the year causes Americans to make the most collect phone calls (where the charges are reversed) to make contact with somebody important. [3]Can you deduce these two holidays and figure out which is which?

Your conclusion: _____

Which sentences have the best evidence to support your conclusion? _____ _____

RHYME TIME

wet	land	bed	hand	pen	call	pop	pet	band
hen	red	ball	bad	hash	lad	bite	drop	bash	night	sand

*Write two rhyming words from the choice box to create a definition
for each item below. Use each choice box word once.*

1. wedding ring _____ _____

2. owned goldfish _____ _____

3. chicken prison _____ _____

4. crimson cot _____ _____

5. naughty boy _____ _____

6. criticize stew _____ _____

7. vampire attack _____ _____

8. desert soil _____ _____

9. spill soda _____ _____

10. umpire decision _____ _____

WHY THE SWITCH TO A REGULAR STAIRWAY?

*Read the true story below, then make an inference
based on the evidence in the story.*

[1]Fires and fire departments have been around for a very long time. [2]By the 19th century firehouses had settled into a logical design. [3]The horses and equipment were housed on the first floor and the sleeping quarters for the firemen were located on the second floor. [4]The two floors were usually connected by a circular staircase. [5]When an alarm went out, the firemen merely had to go downstairs, harness the fire horses to the fire-fighting equipment, and rush off to the fire. [6]Modern firehouses follow this same general design but usually do without the circular staircase. [7]Why did modern firemen switch to a regular stairway?

Your conclusion: _____

Which sentence has the best evidence to support your conclusion? _____

FIGURE OUT THE ORDER

The story below contains events that happened in order. One thing happened first, another second, and so on. Below the story is a chart that lists all the possibilities for each event. Using the clues provided in the story allows you to cross out possibilities under each number until you know the correct order.

FOUR-CAR CRASH

Four cars were involved in a crash on the highway. The first car stopped when the driver spilled hot coffee in his lap and three cars behind him crashed into him or each other. The four cars were a Ford, a Lincoln, a Dodge, and a Jeep. The first car suffered only rear-end damage, the second and third cars received front- and rear-end damage, and the fourth car suffered only front-end damage. The Ford and the Jeep only received damage on one end. The Dodge was struck in the back by the Ford. Place the cars in their correct order in the pileup.

FIRST	SECOND	THIRD	FOURTH
Ford	Ford	Ford	Ford
Lincoln	Lincoln	Lincoln	Lincoln
Dodge	Dodge	Dodge	Dodge
Jeep	Jeep	Jeep	Jeep

1st _____   2nd _____   3rd _____   4th _____

WHAT WAS THIS CHILLY INVENTION?

*Read the true story below, then make an inference
based on the evidence in the story.*

[1]Proving that you don't have to be an adult to come up with a new invention is this story of 11-year-old Frank Epperson. [2]The year was 1905, and it was a bitterly cold day when Frank was enjoying a glass of lemonade. [3]Despite his mother's instructions to finish all his lemonade and clean up after himself, Frank left half a glass of lemonade with a spoon sticking out of it on the windowsill overnight. [4]Years later, Frank Epperson recalled that cold night and his careless actions and received a patent for something he learned from the incident. [5]What did he invent and patent?

Your conclusion: _____

Which sentence has the best evidence to support your conclusion? _____

SPEAKING GERMAN

ice skating	young	better	housewife	broken
dog	foreign	flood	to be sick	serious

*Write the English words from the choice box that best
match the German words below. Some German words are
spelled incorrectly to make them easier to pronounce.*

1. hund   _____

2. jung   _____

3. kaput   _____

4. hausefrau   _____

5. auslandisch   _____

6. besser   _____

7. erkranken   _____

8. eislaufen   _____

9. ernst   _____

10. flut   _____

IN TWO WORDS, IS THERE LIFE ON MARS?

*Read the true story below, then make an inference
based on the evidence in the story.*

[1]William Randolph Hearst was a famous publisher who was always seeking sensational stories. [2]Once the public became interested in the planet Mars and Hearst thought he had a way to cash in on this interest and sell a lot of newspapers. [3]Hearst sought out the most prominent astronomer of the time and offered him a large sum of money if he would write a one-thousand-word essay answering the question, "Is there life on Mars?" [4]The astronomer accepted the deal and replied with a two-word answer repeated five hundred times. [5]What were the two words?

Your conclusion: _____

Which sentence has the best evidence to support your conclusion? _____

WORD CONNECTIONS

trail	party	launch	order	legend
spare	rib	tire	light	tramp

*Write the word from the choice box that best matches the
meaning of both word sets.   Use each choice box word once.*

1. send off   type of boat   _____

2. myth   inscription   _____

3. set on fire   not heavy   _____

4. command   position   _____

5. political group   social gathering   _____

6. tease   chest bone   _____

7. extra part   be merciful   _____

8. become weary   rubber part of wheel   _____

9. hobo   walk heavily   _____

10. path   follow   _____

A UNIQUE 15-LETTER WORD

Read the true story below, then make an inference based on the evidence in the story.

[1]Words with 15 letters are fairly long words, but even so, there are quite a few words in the English language that are 15 letters long. [2]Among these, the word "uncopyrightable" is an oddity. [3]The word, uncopyrightable has one characteristic that sets it apart from all the other 15-letter words in the English language. [4]This unique quality has nothing to do with the meaning of the word and everything to do with how it is spelled. [5]Can you spot the unique characteristic of the word, uncopyrightable?

Your conclusion: _____

Which sentence has the best evidence to support your conclusion? _____

SPEAKING JAPANESE

Australia	boat	aspirin	eat	computer	radiator
	surfboard	engineer	bus	chewing gum	

Write the English words from the choice box that best match the Japanese words below. Some Japanese words are spelled incorrectly to make them easier to pronounce.

1. rajieta   _____

2. boto   _____

3. basu   _____

4. enjinia   _____

5. Osutoraria   _____

6. tabemasu   _____

7. kompyuta   _____

8. chuin gamu   _____

9. asupirin   _____

10. safubodo   _____

J.P. MORGAN'S NOSE

*Read the true story below, then make an inference
based on the evidence in the story.*

[1]J.P. Morgan, in his time, was one of the most powerful men in America. [2]He suffered from rhinophyma, a skin disease that caused his nose to be quite red and swollen. [3]Adults pretended not to notice Morgan's huge honker, but very young children couldn't keep from commenting on his unusual nose. [4]This caused problems for Morgan's younger partners, since he insisted on visiting their homes to meet their wives and children. [5]One young partner's wife very carefully warned their 4-year-old daughter not to say anything about Morgan's enormous red nose when he came to visit. [6]When Morgan arrived to have tea, the young daughter behaved perfectly and was sent off to the nursery. [7]Her very relieved mother then turned to Morgan and asked him if he wanted something very unusual in his tea. [8]What was her question?

Your conclusion: _____

Which sentences have the best evidence to support your conclusion? _____ _____

RHYME TIME

balm	blast	chum	rabbit	damp	glum	bug
glib	habit	creek	camp	dotty	fib	last	try
potty	buy	calm	rug	meek		

*Write two rhyming words from the choice box to create a definition
for each item below. Use each choice box word once.*

1. well-told lie _____ _____

2. final explosion _____ _____

3. gentle stream _____ _____

4. hare custom _____ _____

5. sad friend _____ _____

6. crazy toilet _____ _____

7. carpet insect _____ _____

8. leaky tent _____ _____

9. serene ointment _____ _____

10. make a bid _____ _____

TOSSING CLAY POTS TO WIN THE BATTLE

*Read the true story below, then make an inference
based on the evidence in the story.*

[1]The ancient African city of Carthage fought a series of wars on land and sea against the ancient Italian city of Rome for dominance of the Mediterranean area. [2]Rome eventually defeated Carthage but Carthage had its share of victories along the way. [3]In one sea battle, the Carthaginians used a secret weapon which made use of something Africa had plenty of and Italy had little of to win the battle. [4]The Carthaginians put this something in clay pots, tossed them into Roman ships, and when the clay pots broke, they released whatever was inside. [5]The plan worked perfectly as the Romans were so busy dealing with Carthage's secret weapon that they couldn't fight properly and retreated in great disorder. [6]What was in those clay pots?

Your conclusion: _____

Which sentence has the best evidence to support your conclusion? _____

SPEAKING ITALIAN

one hundred	mother	palace	hobbies	muscle
ugly	boxing	trousers	biscuits	horror

*Write the English words from the choice box that best
match the Italian words below. Some Italian words are
spelled incorrectly to make them easier to pronounce.*

1. pugilato _____

2. pantaloni _____

3. madre _____

4. muscolo _____

5. orrore _____

6. palazzo _____

7. passatempi _____

8. biscotti _____

9. cento _____

10. brutto _____

HER PHOTO IS THE MOST FAMOUS OF ALL

*Read the true story below, then make an inference
based on the evidence in the story.*

[1]There are many people so famous that when we see their pictures we immediately know their names. [2]Usually these are people who are movie stars, television stars, athletes, or politicians. [3]However, few people know the name of Ann Cook and yet her picture is probably the most recognizable of all. [4]Oddly, or perhaps understandably, Ann Cook doesn't even remember when her portrait was made. [5]Today, where will we find Ann Cook's portrait?

Your conclusion: _____

Which sentences have the best evidence to support your conclusion? _____ _____

WHAT'S THE RELATIONSHIP?

*The words in the shaded box have a logical connection to each
other. Circle the word below the shaded box that shares the
relationship. Then explain the relationship between the words.*

1. You are a sight for sore eyes.

mail	trial	Maine	piano

strain   vial   filial

Why? _____

2. "Oh say can you sea…"

Oklahoma	Nevada	Iowa	Indiana

California   Florida   Minnesota

Why? _____

3. Isn't she lovely?

sister	aunt	niece	grandmother

uncle   nephew   mother

Why? _____

AN IMPORTANT SOUNDING SIMPLE DEVICE

*Read the true story below, then make an inference
based on the evidence in the story.*

[1]It seems to be human nature to try to make things seem more important or impressive than they really are. [2]Jobs or objects that perform quite ordinary tasks are given impressive titles or names to make them sound more important. [3]For instance, one company sold an item to the government that was described as a "manually powered fastener-driving impact device." [4]What was this item?

Your conclusion: _____

Which sentence has the best evidence to support your conclusion? _____

FIGURE OUT THE ORDER

*The story below contains events that happened in order. One
thing happened first, another second, and so on. Below the story
is a chart that lists all the possibilities for each event. Using the
clues provided in the story allows you to cross out possibilities
under each number until you know the correct order.*

ORDER OF ABSENCE

Tom, Terry, Thelma, and Talya were each absent from school one day in the same week. None of them was absent on the same day and they all were in school together on Friday. Talya and Terry were not absent on either Monday or Tuesday. Tom missed school later in the week than Thelma and Tom was absent on the day before Talya was absent. Can you figure out the exact day of the week each child was absent?

MONDAY	TUESDAY	WEDNESDAY	THURSDAY
Tom	Tom	Tom	Tom
Terry	Terry	Terry	Terry
Thelma	Thelma	Thelma	Thelma
Talya	Talya	Talya	Talya

Mon. _____   Tues. _____   Wed. _____   Thurs._____

"THE SOUND OF MUSIC" GETS SHORTENED

*Read the true story below, then make an inference
based on the evidence in the story.*

[1]American movies are shown and enjoyed throughout the world but sometimes foreign exhibitors edit out portions of a movie to make it shorter or more acceptable to their local audiences. [2]This often leads to some rather odd results. [3]For instance, there is the case of a South Korean theater manager who decided the musical, "The Sound of Music" was too long and cut out some portions out of the movie. [4]What parts of, "The Sound of Music" did he edit out of the film?

Your conclusion: _____

Which sentence has the best evidence to support your conclusion? _____

WORD CONNECTIONS

lead	refuse	rent	cast	hatch
quiver	part	long	beef	junk

*Write the word from the choice box that best matches the
meaning of both word sets. Use each choice box word once.*

1. throw   actors in a play   _____

2. cow flesh   complaint   _____

3. breed eggs   trapdoor lid   _____

4. Chinese ship   trash   _____

5. heavy metal   guide   _____

6. not short   yearn   _____

7. portion   role in a play   _____

8. shake   arrow case   _____

9. decline   garbage   _____

10. payment for housing   torn   _____

WHAT WAS WRONG WITH REGER'S MUSIC?

*Read the true story below, then make an inference
based on the evidence in the story.*

[1]Critics try to outdo each other in the cleverness of their putdowns. [2]For instance, if someone named "Shorter" makes a movie, you can be sure at least one movie critic will say, "Shorter's movie would be improved by making it like his name... 90 minutes shorter." [3]Something similar happened to the composer Max Reger when one music critic said that Reger's music shared something in common with his last name. [4]Can you guess what the music critic said?

Your conclusion: _____

Which sentence has the best evidence to support your conclusion? _____

SPEAKING FRENCH

ham	wow	four	beer	menu	more
barbershop		painting	bread	sugar	

*Write the English words from the choice box that best
match the French words below. Some French words are
spelled incorrectly to make them easier to pronounce.*

1. carte _____

2. pain _____

3. biere _____

4. sucre _____

5. jambon _____

6. sensass _____

7. tableau _____

8. coiffeur _____

9. encore _____

10. quatre _____

KOREAN DEMONSTRATORS MADE A POINT

*Read the true story below, then make an inference
based on the evidence in the story.*

[1]It is difficult to put a finger on the exact cause of the trouble between Japan and South Korea in 1974, but back then passions were running high. [2]There were large demonstrations in both countries with angry protesters from both sides pointing their fingers at each other. [3]We knew things were getting out of hand when 32 Korean demonstrators did something to themselves to prove how strongly they felt about the dispute. [4]Today, when we cut through the mists of time, we may think their action was pointless, but at the time, it certainly made a splash. [5]Can you guess what these 32 Korean demonstrators did to themselves to prove how strongly they felt about the issue?

Your conclusion: _____

Which sentence has the best evidence to support your conclusion? _____

WHAT'S THE RELATIONSHIP?

*The words in the shaded box have a logical connection to each
other. Circle the word below the shaded box that shares the
relationship. Then explain the relationship between the words.*

1. Lancelot carried a lance.

incompetance	incoherance	independance	interferance

infrequance   insignificance   inheritance

Why?_____

2. Don't go to pieces.

delegate	necklace	potatoes	tearful

lonesome   armament   bride

Why?_____

3. Don't you get it?

moment	papaya	chrysanthemum	doodad

popcorn   smother   confetti

Why? _____

WHAT WERE CHURCHILL AND THE BBC SAYING?

Read the true story below, then make an inference
based on the evidence in the story.

[1]During World War II, British Prime Minister Winston Churchill was often photographed giving a hand gesture with two fingers upraised. [2]Picking up on this theme, the British Broadcasting Company began playing the opening notes of Beethoven's "Fifth Symphony" when it was broadcasting to countries in occupied Europe. [3]The symphony begins with four notes that sound like, "dah, dah, dah, daaah!" [4]What were both Churchill and the BBC saying?

Your conclusion: _____

Which sentences have the best evidence to support your conclusion? _____   _____

SPEAKING ENGLISH

| subway | ice cream sandwich | | picket fence | | druggist | fired |
| closing time | turning signal | | tableware | throat | | retirement |

Write the American words from the choice box that
best match the traditional English words below.

1. slide   _____

2. shutter drill   _____

3. chemist   _____

4. trafficator   _____

5. tube   _____

6. cashiered   _____

7. superannuation   _____

8. throttles   _____

9. crockery   _____

10. paling   _____

ONE NIGHT A YEAR, HE FLIES ALL OVER THE WORLD

Read the true story below, then make an inference
based on the evidence in the story.

[1]In the days of wooden sailing ships, it was quite common for ships to have carved figures on their bows called figureheads. [2]It is reported that the sailing ship that carried the first Dutch settlers to the land we now call New York had a figurehead. [3]This figurehead was that of a character who has become very famous since those early days. [4]One night a year, this character is even said to be seen flying all over the world accompanied by his animals. [5]Who is this character?

Your conclusion: _____

Which sentence has the best evidence to support your conclusion? _____

FIGURE OUT THE ORDER

The story below contains events that happened in order. One
thing happened first, another second, and so on. Below the story
is a chart that lists all the possibilities for each event. Using the
clues provided in the story allows you to cross out possibilities
under each number until you know the correct order.

A MUSICAL DISPUTE

Bill, Bob, Ben, Bev, and Bel were three boys and two girls as shown in order as given in this sentence. They were having an argument over the relative merits of their favorite classical composers. The argument became so intense that one by one they stormed out of the room until the room was empty. None of the children left the room in the same order as they are listed above in the first sentence. Bill left right after the girl who stormed out of the room when Chopin was insulted, but he left the room right before the girl who loved Bach left the room. A boy left the room last, Bel left before Bev, and, of course, Bob left right after Bev stormed out of the room.

FIRST	SECOND	THIRD	FOURTH	FIFTH
Bill	Bill	Bill	Bill	Bill
Bob	Bob	Bob	Bob	Bob
Ben	Ben	Ben	Ben	Ben
Bev	Bev	Bev	Bev	Bev
Bel	Bel	Bel	Bel	Bel

1st _____   2nd _____   3rd _____   4th _____   5tht _____

WHAT ARE THE SIX ROYAL AMERICAN STATES?

*Read the true story below, then make an inference
based on the evidence in the story.*

[1]Six of the United States are named after four British monarchs. [2]These monarchs are King George II, King Charles I, Queen Henrietta Maria, and Queen Elizabeth I. [3]Two of the monarchs had two states named in their honor. [4]Queen Elizabeth I was known as the "virgin queen" because she never married. [5]Can you name all six states?

Your conclusion: _____

Which sentence has the best evidence to support your conclusion? _____

SPEAKING JAPANESE

Europe	hotel	fiction	coffee	ferry
tire	toothbrush	taxi	journalist	hot

*Write the English words from the choice box that best match
the Japanese words below. Some Japanese words are
spelled incorrectly to make them easier to pronounce.*

1. fikushon   _____

2. ha burashi _____

3. kohi   _____

4. atsui   _____

5. yoroppa   _____

6. janarisuto _____

7. takushi   _____

8. feri   _____

9. taiya   _____

10. hoteru   _____

WHO ARE THE FOUR KINGS?

*Read the true story below, then make an inference
based on the evidence in the story.*

[1]In 1952, King Farouk was the last king of Egypt who was forced to give up his throne. [2]When he was king he didn't work very hard and spent much of his time playing cards and pursuing other idle pastimes. [3]King Farouk proved to be quite a joker when he made a prediction as he vacated the throne. [4]He predicted that in a few years time there would be only five kings left in the world. [5]One, he said, would be the King of England. [6]But can you guess who he jokingly predicted would be the remaining four kings?

Your conclusion: _____

Which sentences have the best evidence to support your conclusion? _____ _____

WHAT'S THE RELATIONSHIP?

*The words in the shaded box have a logical connection to each
other. Circle the word below the shaded box that shares the
relationship. Then explain the relationship between the words.*

1. Honk if you know the answer.

bulls	orchestras	rhinoceroses	automobiles

buffaloes   trucks   moose

Why? _____

2. You may find yourself in the middle of some trouble.

throttle	optimist	idealism	abnormal

official   observer   optical

Why? _____

3. Grandmother, such big words you have.

microstomatous	incommensurate	disaffirmation	disapprobation

indifferentism   unintermittent   methodological

Why? _____

WHAT IS THE LAST LETTER?

Read the true story below, then make an inference based on the evidence in the story.

[1]The English language is not an ancient language but has evolved in fairly recent times. The 26th and last letter to be added to the English alphabet was added in the 15th century. [2]It is not the letter "Z". [3]Before this last letter was added, the letter "i" was expected to represent both sounds. [4]The new letter is a consonant and contains a clue that reminds everyone of what its new job was in the alphabet. [5]Can you figure out what the clue is and the last letter to be added to the English alphabet?

Your conclusion: _____

Which sentence has the best evidence to support your conclusion? _____

BEFORE AND AFTER

watch	gum	man	state	family
table	show	room	corn	fly

Write the word from the choice box that makes sense in the blank that appears between the two words or sets of words in each line below. Use each choice box word once.

1. butter _____ fishing

2. Addams _____ feud

3. wrist _____ dog

4. game _____ me the money

5. class _____ with a view

6. chewing _____ drop

7. fire _____ kind

8. secretary of _____ of mind

9. dining room _____ of contents

10. pop _____ on the cob

WHAT TOY WAS TESTED BY THE MILITARY?

*Read the true story below, then make an inference
based on the evidence in the story.*

[1]Every once in awhile something comes along that has a military application that its inventors never considered. [2]For instance, when the airplane was invented, few considered how important it would later become as a weapon of war. [3]In the 1960s, a new toy became popular and the United States military spent a considerable sum of money trying to see if this toy would fly as a military weapon of some sort. [4]What toy was tested for military use and what conclusion did the military reach?

Your conclusion: _____

Which sentence has the best evidence to support your conclusion? _____

FIGURE OUT THE ORDER

The story below contains events that happened in order. One thing happened first, another second, and so on. Below the story is a chart that lists all the possibilities for each event. Using the clues provided in the story allows you to cross out possibilities under each number until you know the correct order.

PIE-EATING CONTEST

Tom, Ted, Terry, Toula, and Tina were the top five finalists in a pie-eating contest. The winner ate 100 pies, second place ate 50 pies, third place ate 25 pies, fourth place ate 15 pies, and fifth place ate only 10 pies. Terry ate twice as many pies as someone else. Toula ate twice as many pies as someone else. Tom ate half as many pies as Toula, and Toula ate five times as many pies as Ted. How did they all finish in the contest? The chart below is organized a bit differently to make the solution easier. Cross out possibilities under the names this time.

TOM	TED	TERRY	TOULA	TINA
100 pies	100 pies	100 pies	100 pies	100 pies
50 pies	50 pies	50 pies	50 pies	50 pies
25 pies	25 pies	25 pies	25 pies	25 pies
15 pies	15 pies	15 pies	15 pies	15 pies
10 pies	10 pies	10 pies	10 pies	10 pies

1st _____ 2nd _____ 3rd _____ 4th _____ 5th _____

THE RECIPE IS IN THE NAME

Read the true story below, then make an inference
based on the evidence in the story.

[1]This familiar baked good took its name from the recipe used in making it. [2]The primary ingredients for this baked good are 16 ounces of sugar, 16 ounces of flour, 16 ounces of eggs, and 16 ounces of butter. [3]What is this baked good called?

Your conclusion: _____

Which sentence has the best evidence to support your conclusion? _____

SPEAKING GERMAN

thanks	laundry	purple	to love	bread
to give	sleeping bag	leather	toothpaste	sugar

Write the English words from the choice box that best
match the German words below. Some German words are
spelled incorrectly to make them easier to pronounce.

1. lieban   _____

2. geban   _____

3. schlafsack _____

4. wascheri   _____

5. brot   _____

6. danke   _____

7. zucker   _____

8. zahnpasta _____

9. leder   _____

10. lila   _____

WHY COULD GREELEY NEVER BE PRESIDENT?

Read the true story below, then make an inference
based on the evidence in the story.

[1]In the 19th century, Horace Greeley was a very famous American. [2]He was a newspaper publisher, an anti-slavery advocate, and finally, he was a presidential candidate. [3]Greeley was the opposition candidate of Ulysses S. Grant when Grant ran for re-election as president in 1872. [4]In the election, Grant received 3,597,132 votes and Greeley received only 2,834,125 votes, making Grant the easy winner. [5]However, shortly after the election something was discovered about Greeley that would have ensured that he would never serve as president even if he had won the election. [6]What was discovered about Greeley that would have prevented him from serving as president?

Your conclusion: _____

Which sentence has the best evidence to support your conclusion? _____

WHAT'S THE RELATIONSHIP?

The words in the shaded box have a logical connection to each
other. Circle the word below the shaded box that shares the
relationship. Then explain the relationship between the words.

1. Double trouble?

cabbage	lessen	pepper	difficult

bubble   irrigate   issue

Why? _____

2. An easy pick.

grappler	sublime	plumage	impeachment

impediment   gluttonous   disappearance

Why? _____

3. Peeling onions makes my eyes water.

striver	bayonet	season	despondent

cloistered   slipstream   futurity

Why? _____

THE FLOWER HAS TEETH!

*Read the true story below, then make an inference
based on the evidence in the story.*

¹One wildflower commonly found in the United States has leaves with notches in them that look like teeth. ²Well, they looked like teeth to the early French explorers who had the honor of naming this plant. ³To the French, these leaves not only looked like teeth, they looked like the teeth of a lion. ⁴Can you figure out what wildflower the French were looking at?

Your conclusion: _____

Which sentence has the best evidence to support your conclusion? _____

SPEAKING JAPANESE

waitress	sign	hockey	department store	knife
celery	shower	dancing	shampoo	mailbox

*Write the English words from the choice box that best match
the Japanese words below. Some Japanese words are
spelled incorrectly to make them easier to pronounce.*

1. shawa _____

2. sain _____

3. yubin posuto _____

4. dansu _____

5. hokke _____

6. depato _____

7. shampu _____

8. naifu _____

9. weitoresu _____

10. serori _____

WHAT'S A GOLFER'S SNOWMAN?

*Read the true story below, then make an inference
based on the evidence in the story.*

[1]Golfers have their own language when it comes to their beloved sport. [2]For instance, a "birdie" is when you finish the hole with one stroke under par. [3]If you finish the hole two strokes under par, it is an even better bird and is called an eagle. [4]How many strokes at the ball did a golfer score when he got what is called a snowman?

Your conclusion: _____

Which sentence has the best evidence to support your conclusion? _____

SPEAKING ENGLISH

dress	junk	stroller		living quarters	umbrella
sweater	streetlight		doll	roll call	suspenders

*Write the American words from the choice box that
best match the traditional English words below.*

1. brolly _____

2. wooly _____

3. braces _____

4. bumf _____

5. frock _____

6. roadlamp _____

7. digs _____

8. callover _____

9. poppet _____

10. push chair _____

WHAT'S THE MEANING OF THAT SCORE?

*Read the true story below, then make an inference
based on the evidence in the story.*

[1]The modern sport of tennis may look quite a bit different from how it looked hundreds of years ago, but the scoring has remained the same over the years. [2]For some reason, scores in tennis are 15 for the first point, 30 for the second point, 40 for the third point, and the last point in a game is the game point. [3]This is where tennis historians begin to bicker over why those numbers are used instead of a more sensible 1, 2, 3, and 4 for the game point. [4]One popular theory is that before the invention of a scoreboard, tennis players used something that was already available and used this device to keep score. [5]Can you guess what this device was that led to the 15, 30, 40, and game-point system?

Your conclusion: _____

Which sentence has the best evidence to support your conclusion? _____

FIGURE OUT THE ORDER

*The story below is about five children who had a contest and finished
in 1st, 2nd, 3rd, 4th, and 5th place based on the number of blisters they
had. The child with the most blisters took 1st place, the child with the
2nd largest number of blisters took 2nd place, and so on. Use the clues
in the story to cross out possibilities in the chart below the story.*

BLISTER CONTEST

Two girls named Anne and Alice and three boys named Art, Al, and Abe went on a charity walkathon. They all developed blisters during the walk and after the walk was over they decided to have a contest based on the number of blisters they each suffered. Of course, first place would be the child with the most blisters and the other places would be determined by the number blisters in descending order. Abe had the fewest blisters of the boys but Abe had more blisters than both of the girls. Al had five times as many blisters as Alice and ten times as many blisters as Anne. Art had four times as many blisters as Alice. You should now be able to figure out the order of finish in the blister contest.

FIRST	SECOND	THIRD	FOURTH	FIFTH
Anne	Anne	Anne	Anne	Anne
Alice	Alice	Alice	Alice	Alice
Art	Art	Art	Art	Art
Al	Al	Al	Al	Al
Abe	Abe	Abe	Abe	Abe

1st _____   2nd _____   3rd _____   4th _____   5th _____

FIRE IN THE LOUVRE!

*Read the true story below, then make an inference
based on the evidence in the story.*

[1]The Louvre in Paris, France, is one of the most famous art museums in the world. [2]It proudly displays perhaps the most famous painting in the world, the "Mona Lisa" by Leonardo Da Vinci. [3]One French newspaper ran a contest trying to spark a lively debate about the merits of the many fine paintings in the museum. [4]Readers would vote on which person came up with the best answer to the question, "If a fire broke out in the Louvre and you could save only one painting, which would it be?" [5]The winner of the contest was Tristan Bernard, who came up with the most sensible answer of all considering the dangers of running into burning buildings. [6]Can you guess Tristan's winning answer?

Your conclusion: _____

Which sentence has the best evidence to support your conclusion? _____

SPEAKING ITALIAN

vote	library	climb	shy	answer
pink	letter	respect	green	school

*Write the English words from the choice box that best
match the Italian words below. Some Italian words are
spelled incorrectly to make them easier to pronounce.*

1. lettera _____

2. libreria _____

3. rosa _____

4. rispetto _____

5. risposta _____

6. scalare _____

7. scuola _____

8. voto _____

9. verde _____

10. timida _____

A STAR PULSING WITH LIFE?

*Read the true story below, then make an inference
based on the evidence in the story.*

[1]In 1967, Antony Hewish and Jocelyn Bell, of Cambridge University in Great Britain, discovered a type of neutron star we now know as a "pulsar." [2]They discovered the pulsar because it gives off a radio wave that is constant in frequency. [3]At first, both Hewish and Bell were very excited because they thought they may have discovered proof of life on other planets. [4]This belief led them to name their discovery LGM-1. [5]The LGM stands for three words often associated with life on other planets. [6]What three words do you think LGM could stand for?

Your conclusion: _____

Which sentence has the best evidence to support your conclusion? _____

BEFORE AND AFTER

chicken	window	sign	code	king
rice	blue	bow	apple	pool

*Write the word from the choice box that makes sense in the
blank that appears between the two words or sets of words
in each line below. Use each choice box word once.*

1. the lion   _____   of hearts

2. bar   _____   of ethics

3. rain   _____   tie

4. fried   _____   pudding

5. swimming   _____   table

6. sky   _____   jeans

7. storm   _____   of opportunity

8. Kentucky fried   _____   of the sea

9. caramel   _____   of my eye

10. neon   _____   language

IN THE MARKET FOR A NEW ROAD

*Read the true story below, then make an inference
based on the evidence in the story.*

[1]New York City was first settled by Dutch settlers from the Netherlands. [2]The Dutch called their settlement "New Amsterdam." [3]In 1653, the Dutch settlers built a stone wall along the northern edge of New Amsterdam as protection against any possible enemies. [4]This stone fence was not very well made and most of it fell down within a few years. [5]Later, the settlers built a road in its place. [6]What did they name the road?

Your conclusion: _____

Which sentences have the best evidence to support your conclusion? _____ _____

SPEAKING GERMAN

| lightning | air mail | church | sausage | tweezers |
| spider | seaweed | cereal | underwear | butterfly |

*Write the English words from the choice box that best
match the German words below. Some German words are
spelled incorrectly to make them easier to pronounce.*

1. pinzette   _____

2. unterwasche   _____

3. musli   _____

4. wurst   _____

5. blitz   _____

6. algen   _____

7. schmetterling   _____

8. spinne   _____

9. kirche   _____

10. luftpost   _____

GOOD SAILORS EAT THEIR VEGETABLES

*Read the true story below, then make an inference
based on the evidence in the story.*

[1]Certain parts of Texas are blessed with a fertile sandy soil that is especially suitable for growing one vegetable in particular. [2]This part of Texas is far from the sea and yet the farmers in this region erected a monument to a famous fictional sailor. [3]Can you guess both the name of this fictional sailor and the vegetable these farmers grew?

Your conclusion: _____

Which sentence has the best evidence to support your conclusion? _____

FIGURE OUT THE ORDER

*The story below is about 5 pigs who held a contest to see
who could drink 5 gallons of swill in the shortest time. The
chart below the story allows you to keep track of the
information by crossing out possibilities under each pig.*

A SWILL CONTEST

Five pigs named Mary, Mildred, Mike, Marty, and Mazie held a swill-gulping contest. The pig who drank 5 gallons of swill in the shortest time would be awarded first place, the pig with the second shortest time would be awarded second place and so on. The times were 10, 15, 20, 24, and 30 seconds. Mary took twice as long to gulp her swill as another pig but so did Mike. Marty took longer to drink his swill than Mary. Mazie took five seconds less than Mary to drink her swill. Use the chart below to cross out answers that don't fit under the name of each pig until you know the correct order.

MARY	MILDRED	MIKE	MARTY	MAZIE
10 seconds	10 seconds	10 seconds	10 seconds	10 seconds
15 seconds	15 seconds	15 seconds	15 seconds	15 seconds
20 seconds	20 seconds	20 seconds	20 seconds	20 seconds
24 seconds	24 seconds	24 seconds	24 seconds	24 seconds
30 seconds	30 seconds	30 seconds	30 seconds	30 seconds

1st _____   2nd _____   3rd _____   4th _____   5th _____

THREE WORDS SAY IT ALL!

*Read the true story below, then make an inference
based on the evidence in the story.*

[1]Camp Fire is an organization similar to the Boy Scouts and Girl Scouts. [2]However, Camp Fire does not separate boys from girls and both will be found in the same group. [3]Camp Fire does separate according to age and has groups such as Sparks, Blue Birds, Adventurers and so on based on age. [4]The Camp Fire watchword is "WOHELO" and is based on three words having to do with labor, physical well-being, and affection. [5]Can you deduce what three words are used to make up the WOHELO watchword?

Your conclusion: _____

Which sentence has the best evidence to support your conclusion? _____

SPEAKING ENGLISH

understand	rich	died	flag	exhausted
loud noise	nonsense	quickly	rude	boss

*Write the American words from the choice box that
best match the traditional English words below.*

1. pranged _____

2. gaffer _____

3. standard _____

4. twaddle _____

5. cheeky _____

6. tumble to _____

7. rowdydow _____

8. knackered _____

9. smartish _____

10. rolling _____

QUIET DOGS LOVE THESE SHOES

*Read the true story below, then make an inference
based on the evidence in the story.*

[1]In 1957, Jim Muir was working for the Wolverine Shoe Company and his job was to come up with a name for a new line of casual shoes that his company was about to start selling. [2]He racked his brain but no name he came up with seemed just right. [3]Finally, an idea came to him when he was enjoying a typical southern-style dinner of deep-fried chicken, deep-fried cornmeal, and deep-fried potatoes. [4]He had coffee and pecan pie for dessert that fortunately weren't deep-fried. [5]What now familiar name for his shoes came to Jim Muir while he was enjoying his southern-style dinner?

Your conclusion: _____

Which sentence has the best evidence to support your conclusion? _____

WHAT'S THE RELATIONSHIP?

*The words in the shaded box have a logical connection to each
other. Circle the word below the shaded box that shares the
relationship. Then explain the relationship between the words.*

1. I question your answer.

petition	inquire	query	ask

interrogate   answer   reply

Why? _____

2. Don't sneak around this one.

boat	coralroot	ladder	aspect

royal   rattletrap   satirical

Why? _____

3. I salute you for getting this one right.

captaincy	privately	admiralty	majority

usually   generally   likely

Why? _____

VOTERS GOT TO WRITE IT IN

*Read the true story below, then make an inference
based on the evidence in the story.*

[1]In 1887, a small community in Arkansas needed to change its name in order to qualify for a post office. [2]The citizens of the town wanted to make this name selection as fair as possible and asked the local school teacher to conduct an election. [3]The school teacher took his job very seriously and tried to make the town name election as foolproof as possible. [4]His ballot came with many instructions for the voters to follow. [5]These included such things as instructions to print clearly in the box provided, do not use a pencil, and to write in ink. [6]What name did the voters select for their town?

Your conclusion: _____

Which sentence has the best evidence to support your conclusion? _____

SPEAKING FRENCH

delete	pill	influenza	save	office supplies
bookstore	emergency	children	stage show	painkiller

*Write the English words from the choice box that best
match the French words below. Some French words are
spelled incorrectly to make them easier to pronounce.*

1. librairie   _____

2. papeterie   _____

3. spectacle   _____

4. sauver   _____

5. annuler   _____

6. enfants   _____

7. urgence   _____

8. la grippe   _____

9. pillule   _____

10. calmant   _____

GREGORY'S DOUGHNUT IMPROVEMENT

Read the true story below, then make an inference
based on the evidence in the story.

[1]According to some published reports, the doughnut was first invented in the Netherlands sometime during the 16th century. [2]The basic doughnut recipe remained relatively unchanged until 1847, when Hanson Gregory is credited with making the first improvement on the basic recipe. [3]Eventually, Hanson's innovation became the standard for the whole world of doughnut makers. [4]What was Hanson's doughnut improvement?

Your conclusion: _____

Which sentence has the best evidence to support your conclusion? _____

FIGURE OUT THE ORDER

The story below contains events that happened in order. In this
case, it involves a car race in which the cars finished in 1, 2, 3 order.
Below the story is a chart that lists all the possibilities for the order of
finish. Using the clues in the story allows you to cross out possibilities
under each number until you can work out the order of finish.

A CLOSE RACE

The top five finishers in the big race were, in no particular order, Car 54, Car 37, Car 31, Car 21, and Car 12. The two cars that shared a second number in common finished in fourth and fifth place. The car with the highest number finished behind the car with the second-highest number. The car with the lowest number finished in front of the car with the second-highest number. The car with the fourth-highest number finished in front of the car with the third-highest number. Now you should know the order of finish in the big race.

FIRST	SECOND	THIRD	FOURTH	FIFTH
Car 54	Car 54	Car 54	Car 54	Car 54
Car 37	Car 37	Car 37	Car 37	Car 37
Car 31	Car 31	Car 31	Car 31	Car 31
Car 21	Car 21	Car 21	Car 21	Car 21
Car 12	Car 12	Car 12	Car 12	Car 12

1st _____ 2nd _____ 3rd _____ 4th _____ 5th _____

A TASTELESS ANCIENT CUSTOM

Read the true story below, then make an inference based on the evidence in the story.

[1]In 1950, the African country of the Ivory Coast was still a colony of France but it had Ivory Coast citizens chosen to represent their country in the French Senate. [2]One such Ivory Coast citizen was Victor Biaka-Boda who had a huge appetite for work and decided to travel to every remote part of the Ivory Coast to meet the people he was representing. [3]Victor Biaka-Boda needed a strong stomach for travel as the Ivory Coast was composed of over 60 distinct tribes with some of them living in very remote areas. [4]One of these tribes that Biaka-Boda visited still followed an ancient custom of dealing with outsiders that unfortunately, caused Victor Biaka-Boda's death. [5]What was this ancient custom?

Your conclusion: _____

Which sentence has the best evidence to support your conclusion? _____

BEFORE AND AFTER

baby	fountain	deck	bag	down
model	box	wheel	diamond	ball

Write the word from the choice box that makes sense in the blank that appears between the two words or sets of words in each line below. Use each choice box word once.

1. shopping _____ of tricks

2. steering _____ of fortune

3. flower _____ of chocolates

4. cry _____ carriage

5. cotton _____ park

6. fashion _____ airplane

7. flight _____ the halls

8. baseball _____ in the rough

9. goose _____ on your luck

10. drinking _____ of youth

SAVE A TOWN — PHILOSOPHICALLY SPEAKING

*Read the true story below, then make an inference
based on the evidence in the story.*

¹In ancient days, Alexander the Great was the greatest conqueror of all time. ²He conquered most of the known world. ³Alexander's usual custom was to destroy any city that dared oppose him and slaughter or enslave its inhabitants. ⁴A Greek philosopher by the name of Anaximenes was Alexander's good friend who traveled with him on his conquests. ⁵Thus, things got a bit tricky when Alexander captured Anaximenes's hometown that contained many of the philosopher's friends and relatives. ⁶So Alexander figured he knew that Anaximenes was going to beg Alexander to spare the town as soon as he saw him. ⁷Before he could open his mouth, Alexander said to Anaximenes, "I have made a vow not to grant your request and you cannot change my mind." ⁸What did Anaximenes then request that saved his hometown from destruction?

Your conclusion: _____

Which sentence has the best evidence to support your conclusion? _____

SPEAKING GERMAN

false	hairbrush	behind	cuckoo clock	alarm clock
raincoat	coat	dark	dancing	garden

*Write the English words from the choice box that best
match the German words below. Some German words are
spelled incorrectly to make them easier to pronounce.*

1. hinter   _____

2. wecker   _____

3. mantel   _____

4. dunkel   _____

5. tanzen   _____

6. falsch   _____

7. garten   _____

8. haarburste   _____

9. kuckucksuhr   _____

10. regenmantel   _____

THIS RUNS HOT AND COLD

Read the true story below, then make an inference
based on the evidence in the story.

[1]Most sinks today around the world follow the same pattern with the cold water knob on the right and the hot water knob on the left. [2]There is a logical reason for this and it dates back to the time when running water was first introduced into the home. [3]A later second invention was responsible for the standard hot/cold knob arrangement. [4]Can you think what it was?

Your conclusion: _____

Which sentence has the best evidence to support your conclusion? _____

SPEAKING ENGLISH

installment plan	risky	killer	naked	tongue
fingerprints	selling	promotion	sideways	clothespins

Write the American words from the choice box that
best match the traditional English words below.

1. starkers   _____

2. edgeways   _____

3. pegs   _____

4. never-never   _____

5. red rag   _____

6. dicey   _____

7. dabs   _____

8. elevation   _____

9. flogging   _____

10. croaker   _____

NOT SUCH A GOOD SINGER?

*Read the true story below, then make an inference
based on the evidence in the story.*

[1]Guido Nazzo was an Italian tenor who was fairly popular in Italy more than 70 years ago. [2]He decided to tour the United States and showcase his singing talents but his first concert in New York received a devastating review from a music critic. [3]The review consisted of only four words. [4]The first two words of the review were, "Guido Nazzo." [5]If you are a pun-loving type of person you should be able to figure out what the next two words of the review were. [6]If you don't like puns then the odds are not so good that you will figure out the answer.

Your conclusion: _____

Which sentence has the best evidence to support your conclusion? _____

SPEAKING FRENCH

| light | carry | food | toothpaste | great |
| dangerous | candle | ask | cat | hairbrush |

*Write the English words from the choice box that best
match the French words below. Some French words are
spelled incorrectly to make them easier to pronounce.*

1. dentifrice _____

2. brosse _____

3. formidable _____

4. nourriture _____

5. dangereux _____

6. chat _____

7. blonde _____

8. demander _____

9. chandelle _____

10. porter _____

TIME TO SEE THE LIGHT!

*Read the true story below, then make an inference
based on the evidence in the story.*

[1]Traffic signals in the United States are important safety devices designed to protect lives and property. [2]The lights are always red on top, yellow in the middle, and green on the bottom. [3]Traffic safety experts believe it is important that this red-yellow-green pattern never be changed in order to protect us from what kind of people?

Your conclusion: _____

Which sentence has the best evidence to support your conclusion? _____

FIGURE OUT THE ORDER

The story below contains events that happened in order. One thing happened first, another second, and so on. Below the story is a chart that lists all the possibilities for each event. Using the clues provided in the story allows you to cross out possibilities until you know the correct sequence of events.

HEY, HEY WE'RE THE MONKEYS!

One day, five monkeys named Bosco, Tippi, Lena, Ralph, and Lance were playing in a tree together. They were careless and one by one they all managed to fall out of the tree. Lance, Tippi, and Ralph were not among the first two to fall out of the tree. Tippi laughed so hard when she saw Ralph fall out of the tree that she fell out of the tree herself right after Ralph. There was at least one other monkey in the tree who laughed when Tippi fell out of the tree, and Bosco was still in the tree when Lena fell out of the tree. Now you should know in what order the monkeys fell out of the tree.

FIRST	SECOND	THIRD	FOURTH	FIFTH
Bosco	Bosco	Bosco	Bosco	Bosco
Tippi	Tippi	Tippi	Tippi	Tippi
Lena	Lena	Lena	Lena	Lena
Ralph	Ralph	Ralph	Ralph	Ralph
Lance	Lance	Lance	Lance	Lance

1st _____ 2nd _____ 3rd _____ 4th _____ 5th _____

GETTING AROUND TO MOVING THE COVERS

*Read the true story below, then make an inference
based on the evidence in the story.*

[1]Those heavy metal covers for drainage or sewer systems can come in all sizes and shapes. [2]However, the most popular shape is the round shape. [3]People who work on these systems who have to occasionally remove these covers prefer to work with round-shaped drainage covers as well. [4]Why do you suppose the experts prefer round drainage-system covers?

Your conclusion: _____

Which sentence has the best evidence to support your conclusion? _____

SPEAKING FRENCH

song	light	delay	boiled	help
fight	trout	scissors	occupation	face

*Write the English words from the choice box that best
match the French words below. Some French words are
spelled incorrectly to make them easier to pronounce.*

1. retardement _____

2. visage _____

3. combattre _____

4. secours _____

5. lumiere _____

6. emploi _____

7. ciseaux _____

8. chanson _____

9. bouill _____

10. truite _____

GETTING OFF ON THE RIGHT FOOT

*Read the true story below, then make an inference
based on the evidence in the story.*

[1]One modern tradition dates back to the time of the ancient Romans. [2]The Romans had a strong belief that you had to always enter a house with your right foot first or you would be inviting evil spirits into the house. [3]All Romans of every age and gender was trusted to follow this rule. [4]The only exception to this rule was one day in a woman's life when nobody trusted her to enter a room properly with her right foot first. [5]What was that day and what tradition did it lead to that is still practiced today?

Your conclusion: _____

Which sentence has the best evidence to support your conclusion? _____

SPEAKING JAPANESE

e-mail	rainy	tiger	visa	orange
litter	rules	picnic	pump	lemonade

*Write the English words from the choice box that best match
the Japanese words below. Some Japanese words are
spelled incorrectly to make them easier to pronounce.*

1. orenji   _____

2. remonedo   _____

3. ame   _____

4. i meru   _____

5. rittoru   _____

6. tora   _____

7. ruru   _____

8. pikunikku   _____

9. biza   _____

10. pompu   _____

IF THE SHOE FITS, STOP LOAFING AROUND

*Read the true story below, then make an inference
based on the evidence in the story.*

[1]Many countries in Europe have a long tradition of having a large fishing industry.
[2]England, Scotland, Sweden, Norway, Denmark, Germany, the Netherlands, Russia,
and Iceland are some of them. [3]But the fishermen of only one of these countries has a
still-popular shoe style named after them. [4]"Weejuns" were inspired by a shoe worn by
fishermen from which of the named countries?

Your conclusion: _____

Which sentence has the best evidence to support your conclusion? _____

SPEAKING ITALIAN

hat	refuse	lightbulb	greedy	gardens
to dance	detergent	big	sculpture	traffic lights

*Write the English words from the choice box that best
match the Italian words below. Some Italian words are
spelled incorrectly to make them easier to pronounce.*

1. semaforo   _____

2. scultura   _____

3. rifiutare   _____

4. grande   _____

5. lampardina   _____

6. avida   _____

7. ballare   _____

8. detersivo   _____

9. giardini   _____

10. cappello   _____

A GREAT DOOR OPENER

Read the true story below, then make an inference
based on the evidence in the story.

[1]There are distinct advantages to having a door to the outside that opens inward rather than outward. [2]For instance, if your front door or back door has storm doors, the storm doors would have to open outward or you could never open them from the outside. [3]Another advantage is that doors that open inwards have their hinges on the inside so they are not exposed to the weather and they are unavailable to burglars who could break the hinges to gain entry. [4]Despite these advantages, the doors to most public building such as restaurants or stores open outward. [5]Why do you suppose this is?

Your conclusion: _____

Which sentence has the best evidence to support your conclusion? _____

SPEAKING GERMAN

teacher	comedy	fresh	to have	style
kiss	cat	good	to win	children

Write the English words from the choice box that best
match the German words below. Some German words are
spelled incorrectly to make them easier to pronounce.

1. frisch _____

2. gewinnen _____

3. haben _____

4. gut _____

5. katze _____

6. kinder _____

7. komodie _____

8. kussen _____

9. stil _____

10. lehrer _____

HORSES IN GOOD STANDING

*Read the true story below, then make an inference
based on the evidence in the story.*

[1]Horses are herd animals and generally like to hang out close to each other. [2]Chances are, if you see two horses in a field after they have finished grazing, they will be found standing next to each other. [3]However, during warm weather, they will usually be seen standing head to tail and during cold weather, they will usually stand head to head. [4]Can you figure out why they switch positions during different seasons?

Your conclusion: _____

Which sentence has the best evidence to support your conclusion? _____

RHYME TIME

mobster	gull	fine	mellow	trove	lazy	dull
silly	fellow	grove	daisy	billy	shovel	lobster
louder	doggy	hovel	chowder	brine	foggy	

*Write two rhyming words from the choice box to create a definition
for each item below. Use each choice box word once.*

1. foolish goat _____   _____

2. boring seabird _____   _____

3. cloudy canine _____   _____

4. spade shack _____   _____

5. excellent seawater _____   _____

6. noisier soup _____   _____

7. Crustacean criminal _____   _____

8. relaxed man _____   _____

9. forest treasure _____   _____

10. shiftless flower _____   _____

IT'S TIME TO THROW THESE OUT!

Read the true story below, then make an inference
based on the evidence in the story.

[1]Few people have heard of Marion Donovan yet the product she invented back in 1951 is sold by the millions every day. [2]Those who purchase the product are older than those who actually use the product. [3]As soon as the product is used it is immediately thrown away by the person who bought the product in the first place. [4]What is this product?

Your conclusion: _____

Which sentence has the best evidence to support your conclusion? _____

FIGURE OUT THE ORDER

The story below contains a story about a fly-eating contest between five frogs. Your assignment is to read the story and use the clues to determine how many flies each frog ate. Below the story is a chart which lists all the possibilities. Use the clues in the story to cross out possibilities under each name until you know the answer.

FLY-EATING CONTEST

Belle, Benny, Byron, Bonnie, and Boris were five frogs who entered a fly-eating contest to see who could eat the most flies in a minute. They ate 250, 200, 125, 100, and 50 flies in a minute. Benny, Bonnie, and Boris all ate twice as many flies as another frog. Byron ate more flies than both Belle and Boris, but Byron only ate half as many flies as Bonnie. Now you can determine how many flies each frog ate and their order of finish in the contest.

BELLE	BENNY	BYRON	BONNIE	BORIS
250	250	250	250	250
200	200	200	200	200
125	125	125	125	125
100	100	100	100	100
50	50	50	50	50

1st _____   2nd _____   3rd _____   4th _____   5th _____

SPELLING OUT THE SECRET GROUP

*Read the true story below, then make an inference
based on the evidence in the story.*

[1]A fairly recent addition to the English language is the word "cabal," which refers to any small group of people who join together in secret to accomplish their goals. [2]The word dates back to the reign of King Charles II (1630-95) of England and his Privy Council. [3]Their names were Arlington, Ashley, Buckingham, Clifford, and Lauderdale. [4]How did the word cabal come to be invented?

Your conclusion: _____

Which sentence has the best evidence to support your conclusion? _____

SPEAKING ENGLISH

wind gust	two weeks	bacon	excited	renter
dusk	expert	scatterbrained	drudge	warehouse

*Write the American words from the choice box that
best match the traditional English words below.*

1. streaky _____

2. dogsbody _____

3. scatty _____

4. nervy _____

5. stores _____

6. lodger _____

7. scud _____

8. evenfall _____

9. fortnight _____

10. boffin _____

PRETTY BUT WORTHLESS TREASURES

*Read the true story below, then make an inference
based on the evidence in the story.*

[1]Neptune was the god of the sea in the ancient Roman religion. [2]Caligula was the Roman Emperor from the years 12 to 41 A.D. and was considered to be quite crazy. [3]At one time he even made his horse a member of the Roman Senate. [4]For some reason he became angry at Neptune and declared war on him. [5]Caligula marched his army down to the sea and had his soldiers run into the water stabbing it with their swords. [6]When he decided Neptune had had enough, Caligula declared victory and took away some of Neptune's treasures in large chests. [7]What was Neptune's treasure to Caligula's rather deranged way of thinking?

Your conclusion: _____

Which sentences have the best evidence to support your conclusion? _____ _____

SPEAKING ITALIAN

salary	nothing	good night	teacher	hungry
driver	business	misery	quiet	friend

*Write the English words from the choice box that best
match the Italian words below. Some Italian words are
spelled incorrectly to make them easier to pronounce.*

1. nulla   _____

2. infelicita   _____

3. silenziosa   _____

4. buonanotte   _____

5. amica   _____

6. economia   _____

7. professore   _____

8. lo stipendio _____

9. fame   _____

10. l'autista   _____

OBIE ONE, OBIE TWO

*Read the true story below, then make an inference
based on the evidence in the story.*

[1]Oddly enough, Obie is the name of two completely different awards given out each year. [2]The most widely known Obie is an award for Off-Broadway plays and performances in New York. [3]The name Obie is derived from the initials in the words Off-Broadway. [4]The second Obie is an outdoor advertising business award also derived from the first two initials in the name of the type of business being honored. [5]The founders of this award also claim that the Obie is based on the original function of the Egyptian obelisk which was a tall tower covered with Egyptian picture writing. [6]What business is this second Obie honoring?

Your conclusion: _____

Which sentence has the best evidence to support your conclusion? _____

SPEAKING JAPANESE

party	matches	shower	page	cabbage
lemonade	film	towel	size	poster

*Write the English words from the choice box that best match
the Japanese words below. Some Japanese words are
spelled incorrectly to make them easier to pronounce.*

1. peji _____

2. posuta _____

3. shawa _____

4. taoru _____

5. saizu _____

6. firumu _____

7. macchi _____

8. pati _____

9. kyabetsu _____

10. remonedo _____

LOOK UP! WHAT'S THAT IN THE SKY?

*Read the true story below, then make an inference
based on the evidence in the story.*

[1]Different cultures have different, often descriptive, names for the same natural phenomena. [2]For instance, the Italians call it, "the flashing arch." [3]In Sanskrit, it is called "the Bow of Indra." [4]The people of Annam called it, "the little window in the sky!" [5]What do we call it?

Your conclusion: _____

Which sentences have the best evidence to support your conclusion? _____   _____

SPEAKING FRENCH

party	cake		daughter	ship	muggy
asparagus		city	luggage	helpful	lemon

*Write the English words from the choice box that best
match the French words below. Some French words are
spelled incorrectly to make them easier to pronounce.*

1. asperges _____

2. gateau _____

3. citron _____

4. ville _____

5. fille _____

6. humide _____

7. serviable _____

8. bagage _____

9. soiree _____

10. navire _____

THE RAFFEL BROTHERS' RESTAURANT

*Read the true story below, then make an inference
based on the evidence in the story.*

[1]In 1964, Forrest Raffel and his brother, LeRoy, decided to start a restaurant together. [2]They had a good idea and the restaurant became so popular that they decided to franchise more restaurants based on their first restaurant. [3]They named this first restaurant after themselves and now restaurants with this original name can be found all over the country. [4]Name this fast-food chain founded by Forrest and LeRoy Raffel.

Your conclusion: _____

Which sentences have the best evidence to support your conclusion? _____ _____

RHYME TIME

tingle	rooter	coach	loaves	single	least
mash	cooler	clean	beast	tooter	jeweler	rare
roach	meal	stoves	bean	trash	bear	real

*Write two rhyming words from the choice box to create a
definition for each item below. Use each choice box word once.*

1. fan trumpeter   _____   _____

2. smallest lion   _____   _____

3. spotless legume   _____   _____

4. calmer goldsmith   _____   _____

5. compact garbash   _____   _____

6. one chill   _____   _____

7. unusual grizzly   _____   _____

8. insect trainer   _____   _____

9. genuine dinner   _____   _____

10. bread ovens   _____   _____

IT'S A SMALL WORLD

*Read the true story below, then make an inference
based on the evidence in the story.*

[1]In 1951, the St. Louis Browns baseball team was the worst team in major league baseball. [2]They were so bad that it was unusual for them to even get a man on base much less score a run. [3]Finally, they hired a man by the name of Eddie Gaedel to play for their team figuring that he was almost certain to get on base every time he came up to the plate. [4]The first time Mr. Gaedel was at bat, he got on first base and things seemed to be looking up for the hapless Browns. [5]However, two days after his first appearance in a Browns uniform, the commissioner of baseball banned Eddie Gaedel from ever playing major league baseball again. [6]The commissioner went even farther and banned anyone who even looked like Eddie Gaedel from playing major league baseball. [7]What did the baseball commissioner have against Eddie Gaedel?

Your conclusion: _____

Which sentences have the best evidence to support your conclusion? _____ _____

FIGURE OUT THE ORDER

The story below concerns a contest between five gorillas to see who could stuff the most grapes in their cheeks. Your assignment is to read the story and figure out how many grapes each of the gorillas stuffed in their cheeks. Below the story is a chart that lists all the possibilities. Use the clues in the story to cross out possibilities under each gorilla until you know the answer.

A GRAPE CONTEST

Bingo, Bongo, Tango, Koko, and Chico were five gorillas who decided to hold a contest to see who could stuff the most grapes in their cheeks. They stuffed 75, 70, 65, 40, and 35 grapes in their cheeks. Bongo, Tango, and Chico all managed to stuff exactly 5 more grapes in their cheeks than the gorillas who finished one place behind them. Bingo stuffed exactly 10 fewer grapes in his cheeks than Tango. Chico didn't stuff as many grapes in his cheeks as Bongo.

BINGO	BONGO	TANGO	KOKO	CHICO
75	75	75	75	75
70	70	70	70	70
65	65	65	65	65
40	40	40	40	40
35	35	35	35	35

1st _____ 2nd _____ 3rd _____ 4th _____ 5th _____

IS IT TRUE CATS HAVE NINE LIVES?

*Read the true story below, then make an inference
based on the evidence in the story.*

[1]In 1989, it was reported in the *New York Times* weekly science supplement that researchers had discovered cats have the remarkable ability to survive falls from great heights. [2]Researchers interviewed New York veterinarians and discovered that 132 cats had survived falls from apartment buildings in just one five-month period. [3]Later, the *New York Times* had to write a correction to this story because cats have no more ability to survive falls from great heights than any other animal of the same size. [4]If you think about it, veterinarians are exactly the wrong people to answer this question. [5]Why?

Your conclusion: _____

Which sentences have the best evidence to support your conclusion? _____ _____

RHYME TIME

yield	jar	ample	cotton	wandering	lamp	crone
far	meal	rotten	candy	deal	belly	field	damp
	stone	smelly	handy	pondering	sample	

*Write two rhyming words from the choice box to create a definition
for each item below. Use each choice box word once.*

1. distant container   _____   _____

2. rock witch   _____   _____

3. big taste   _____   _____

4. odiferous stomach   _____   _____

5. lunch bargain   _____   _____

6. decayed cloth   _____   _____

7. wayward thinking   _____   _____

8. wet light   _____   _____

9. crop production   _____   _____

10. useful treat   _____   _____

EGADS! IT'S MISSING!

Read the true story below, then make an inference
based on the evidence in the story.

[1]What is unusual about a fifty-thousand-word book in print in 1937 known as "Gadsby"? [2]It is unusual in a way similar to this paragraph, which lacks a thing found in most books or in any dictionary. [3]It is not difficult if your brain is working today. [4]What was missing from "Gadsby" and is missing from this paragraph?

Your conclusion: _____

Which sentence has the best evidence to support your conclusion? _____

BEFORE AND AFTER

command	rise	soap	bonds	light
gum	fire	button	one	wet

Write the word from the choice box that makes sense in the
blank that appears between the two words or sets of words
in each line below. Use each choice box word once.

1. bar of _____ opera

2. forest _____ works

3. savings _____ of matrimony

4. chewing _____ up the works

5. traffic _____ as a feather

6. chain of _____ performance

7. slippery when _____ your whistle

8. hole in _____ of a kind

9. panic _____ mushrooms

10. sun _____ and shine

LET'S BE MORE ENTHUSIASTIC!

Read the true story below, then make an inference
based on the evidence in the story.

[1]The American movie star Warren Beatty once produced a movie based on the life of the journalist John Reed who was famous for his praise of the Russian Revolution. [2]The movie had many extras and Warren Beatty was concerned that they weren't showing enough emotion about the rights of the working man who was very enthusiastic about the revolution when it began. [3]Warren Beatty gave a speech to the extras in which he told them how the workers at the time were downtrodden and the revolution gave them hope that conditions would improve. [4]Warren Beatty then left the meeting and told the extras to discuss what he had said. [5]What was the result of this discussion which made Warren Beatty sorry he called the meeting in the first place?

Your conclusion: _____

Which sentences have the best evidence to support your conclusion? _____ _____

SPEAKING CZECH

restaurant	asthma	OK	custard	son
check	television	salad	mayonnaise	wine

Write the English words from the choice box that best
match the Czech words below. Some Czech words are
spelled incorrectly to make them easier to pronounce.

1. fain _____

2. majoneza _____

3. salat _____

4. vino _____

5. astma _____

6. bufet _____

7. sek _____

8. sin _____

9. televize _____

10. pudink _____

NO LUNCH BOX IS COMPLETE WITHOUT IT

Read the true story below, then make an inference
based on the evidence in the story.

[1]James Dewar was an English chemist in the 19th century. [2]He was working with chemicals trying to discover how cold affected their properties. [3]His trouble was trying to keep the chemicals cold while he conducted his experiments. [4]He decided he needed a container that would keep the chemicals he was working with cold for a long time. [5]He designed just such a container and in doing so made a useful invention. [6]What did James Dewar invent?

Your conclusion: _____

Which sentence has the best evidence to support your conclusion? _____

SPEAKING HUNGARIAN

vase	fan	light	lemonade		towel
bellhop	mailbox	accelerator		terrace	clock

Write the English words from the choice box that best match
the Hungarian words below. Some Hungarian words are
spelled incorrectly to make them easier to pronounce.

1. gazpedal _____

2. ventillator _____

3. lampa _____

4. postalada _____

5. boyt _____

6. torulkozot _____

7. ora _____

8. teresz _____

9. vaza _____

10. limonadet _____

FISHY DESIGNS IN BATHROOM SHOWERS

*Read the true story below, then make an inference
based on the evidence in the story.*

[1]Among the rich mosaic of marine life, the most colorfully decorated ocean fish to be found in northern waters is a species than can grow to 3 feet in length and weigh 30 pounds or more. [2]It received its name because of its beautiful coloring that includes blue, green, rose, red, yellow, and white markings. [3]Some makers of ceramic products have even been inspired to create designs that resemble the color scheme of this beautiful fish. [4]What is the logical name of this decorative fish?

Your conclusion: _____

Which sentence has the best evidence to support your conclusion? _____

SPEAKING TURKISH

movie theater	newspaper	flu	suitcase	bus
gas station	ticket	campsite	gallery	toilet

*Write the English words from the choice box that best
match the Turkish words below. Some Turkish words are
spelled incorrectly to make them easier to pronounce.*

1. valiz   _____

2. gazete   _____

3. grip   _____

4. tuvalet   _____

5. galerisi   _____

6. kamp yeri   _____

7. otobus   _____

8. sinema   _____

9. benzin deposu _____

10. bilet   _____

SEW, A NEEDLE PULLING THREAD

*Read the true story below, then make an inference
based on the evidence in the story.*

[1]There is a songbird native to China, India, Malaysia, and the Philippines that builds its nest in an unusual fashion. [2]The bird folds a large leaf in half and then sews the edges of the leaf together with pieces of fiber, using its bill as a needle. [3]What is the name of this clever songbird?

Your conclusion: _____

Which sentence has the best evidence to support your conclusion? _____

SPEAKING RUSSIAN

rackets	third	July	map	flu	lip balm
	Greece	zoo	concert	toilet	

*Write the English words from the choice box that best match
the Russian words below. Some of the Russian words are
spelled phonetically to make them easier to pronounce.*

1. krem dlya gup _____

2. gripa _____

3. karta _____

4. Gryetsiya _____

5. Eeyul _____

6. tryetii _____

7. tualyet _____

8. rakyetki _____

9. kantsert _____

10. zaapark _____

IT'S NOT A NIGHT OWL FLOWER

*Read the true story below, then make an inference
based on the evidence in the story.*

¹One type of lily grows clusters of flowers on stalks that grow 3 to 5 feet high. ²The flowers are either yellow or orange and each cluster grows 6 to 12 flowers.   ³Of the flowers in each cluster, two or three open each day but only live from sunrise to sunset before dying. ⁴What is the name given to this kind of lily?

Your conclusion: _____

Which sentence has the best evidence to support your conclusion? _____

SPEAKING SWAHILI

battery	bus	receipt	seventy	diesel
Internet	elevator	hello	cabin	newspaper

*Write the English words from the choice box that best
match the Swahili words below. Some Swahili words are
spelled incorrectly to make them easier to pronounce.*

1. habari   _____

2. sabini   _____

3. risiti   _____

4. basi   _____

5. kibini   _____

6. dizeli   _____

7. betri   _____

8. lifti   _____

9. gazeti   _____

10. Intaneti   _____

AND THE WINNER IS...

*Read the true story below, then make an inference
based on the evidence in the story.*

[1]We all have heard of the "Oscar," which is the name given to an Academy Award. [2]However, there is another coveted film award with a different name. [3]An international film society gives out an annual award called an "Annie." [4]The Annie awards are the highest honor given for excellence in the making of what kind of film?

Your conclusion: _____

Which sentence has the best evidence to support your conclusion? _____

RHYME TIME

Bill	city	straight	buddy	cattle	candy	mire
fix	carriage	ruddy	biddy	battle	handy	eight
marriage	Bics	desire	fountain	spill	mountain	

*Write two rhyming words from the choice box to create a definition
for each item below. Use each choice box word once.*

1. red-faced pal   _____   _____

2. unbent number   _____   _____

3. buggy wedlock   _____   _____

4. mend ballpoints   _____   _____

5. crave mud   _____   _____

6. overturn William   _____   _____

7. peak waterworks   _____   _____

8. urban old lady   _____   _____

9. cows warfare   _____   _____

10. available sweets   _____   _____

THEY LEAVE NO STONE UNTURNED

*Read the true story below, then make an inference
based on the evidence in the story.*

[1]There are two kinds of birds that belong to the sandpiper family which share the same name. [2]They received their name because they search for food by flipping stones over with their bills and eating anything that might be hiding under the stones. [3]These are not to be confused with terns, which are a different type of sea bird entirely. [4]What name do they share based on how they search for food?

Your conclusion: _____

Which sentence has the best evidence to support your conclusion? _____

SPEAKING CZECH

Europe	milk	bus	weekend	water
photograph	tennis court	alcohol	Saturday	garage

*Write the English words from the choice box that best
match the Czech words below. Some Czech words are
spelled incorrectly to make them easier to pronounce.*

1. voda   _____

2. vikend   _____

3. Evropa   _____

4. fotka   _____

5. mleko   _____

6. autobus   _____

7. Sobota   _____

8. alkohol   _____

9. kurt   _____

10. garaz   _____

THAT'S QUITE A MONKEY'S TALE

*Read the true story below, then make an inference
based on the evidence in the story.*

[1]Experts believe one of the letters in our alphabet began about 5,000 years ago as an Egyptian picture of a monkey. [2]Over the centuries the letter started to look less and less like a monkey until it reached its final shape under the Romans in about A.D. 114. [3]The only thing the Romans kept from the original Egyptian monkey was its tail. [4]What letter are we talking about?

Your conclusion: _____

Which sentences have the best evidence to support your conclusion? _____ _____

SPEAKING TURKISH

museum	heater	postcard	lipstick	cab
cake shop	balcony	tea	water	train

*Write the English words from the choice box that best
match the Turkish words below. Some Turkish words are
spelled incorrectly to make them easier to pronounce.*

1. pastane _____

2. muze _____

3. taksi _____

4. trene _____

5. balkonlu _____

6. cay _____

7. su _____

8. kalorifer _____

9. ruj _____

10. kartpostal _____

A BUGGY SMELL

*Read the true story below, then make an inference
based on the evidence in the story.*

[1]There is a family of insects that sprays a foul-smelling odor from scent glands located near their hind legs or on their abdomens when they are frightened by possible predators. [2]This bad-smelling odor signals to all that they would not be good to eat and these insects are allowed to go about their business undisturbed. [3]By what logical name do we know these clever bugs?

Your conclusion: _____

Which sentence has the best evidence to support your conclusion? _____

SPEAKING RUSSIAN

engine	hello	radio	address	ticket
swimming pool	airport	passport	Canada	airmail

*Write the English words from the choice box that best
match the Russian words below. Some Russian words are
spelled incorrectly to make them easier to pronounce.*

1. bilyeta   _____

2. basein   _____

3. airavakzdla   _____

4. mator   _____

5. alyo   _____

6. paspart   _____

7. avia   _____

8. Kanadai   _____

9. tranzister   _____

10. adris   _____

THIS RECORD WILL NEVER BE BROKEN

*Read the true story below, then make an inference
based on the evidence in the story.*

[1]It is considered a great achievement to win an Olympic medal in any sport either in the summer or winter games. [2]In 1988, a female athlete from East Germany won an Olympic medal in the summer sport of cycling and in that same year won an Olympic medal in the winter sport of speed skating. [3]Since then, everyone agrees, no athlete will ever duplicate this feat of winning an Olympic medal in both the winter and summer games in the same year. [4]Why does everyone agree that this feat is impossible?

Your conclusion: _____

Which sentences have the best evidence to support your conclusion? _____ _____

SPEAKING HUNGARIAN

blouse	sugar	ceramics	fresh	lemon
potato salad	campsite	mayonnaise	pajamas	jacket

*Write the English words from the choice box that best match
the Hungarian words below. Some Hungarian words are
spelled incorrectly to make them easier to pronounce.*

1. friss   _____

2. majonez   _____

3. cukor   _____

4. krumplisalata _____

5. citrom   _____

6. kemping   _____

7. bluz   _____

8. zako   _____

9. pizsama   _____

10. keramia   _____

THOSE RICH ELEMENTS

*Read the true story below, then make an inference
based on the evidence in the story.*

[1]Some names of things don't make any sense unless you understand the historical context of when they were named. [2]During the 1890s, Great Britain was a society in which the class system was very strong. [3]The upper classes such as the nobility didn't have anything to do with those who belonged to the lower classes and it was considered improper for any of the classes to either step above or below their stations in life and socialize with each other. [4]During this time, the chemical elements of argon, helium, krypton, neon, radon, and xenon were discovered. [5]Why do we call them the "noble gases" today?

Your conclusion: _____

Which sentence has the best evidence to support your conclusion? _____

SPEAKING SWAHILI

apartment	America	towel	cobra	bath
golf course	week	budget	ambulance	Band-Aid

*Write the English words from the choice box that best
match the Swahili words below. Some Swahili words are
spelled incorrectly to make them easier to pronounce.*

1. taulo _____

2. wa gofu _____

3. wiki _____

4. gari la hospitall _____

5. Marekani _____

6. fleti _____

7. Elasto _____

8. bafu _____

9. bajeti _____

10. koboko _____

HERE'S HOPING YOU CAN NAME THAT CAPE

*Read the true story below, then make an inference
based on the evidence in the story.*

[1]When sailing west to the Americas from England, the last sight of land is a cape that sticks out into the English Channel where it opens up into the Atlantic Ocean. [2]Over the centuries, sailors gave this cape a descriptive two-word name. [3]Many years after it was named, someone thought it would be a great name for a chain of clothing stores. [4]What is the two-word name of this famous cape?

Your conclusion: _____

Which sentences have the best evidence to support your conclusion? _____   _____

SPEAKING CZECH

home	Asia	movies	coach	guitar
thirty	telephone	toilets	volleyball	none

*Write the English words from the choice box that best
match the Czech words below. Some Czech words are
spelled incorrectly to make them easier to pronounce.*

1. Asie   _____

2. tricet   _____

3. nic   _____

4. telepfonni   _____

5. volejbal   _____

6. trener   _____

7. toalety   _____

8. filmy   _____

9. domov   _____

10. kytara   _____

THIS MILK'S FOR THE BIRDS

Read the true story below, then make an inference
based on the evidence in the story.

[1]There is a type of bird that received its name based on false evidence but that doesn't stop us from continuing to use it. [2]This bird has a wide, soft mouth instead of a sharp beak and was often seen flying around at night close to herds of goats. [3]Observing this behavior and noting the type of mouth these birds have, people assumed these birds were landing at night and stealing the milk from female goats. [4]We now know the birds have wide, soft mouths useful for swallowing flying insects and, of course, they were flying near goat herds because goats attract insects. [5]What is the common name for this type of bird?

Your conclusion: _____

Which sentence has the best evidence to support your conclusion? _____

SPEAKING TURKISH

sponge	blue color	flash bulbs	jacket	tart
bread	jeans	tailored suit	pipe tobacco	disinfectant

Write the English words from the choice box that best
match the Turkish words below. Some Turkish words are
spelled incorrectly to make them easier to pronounce.

1. flas lambasi _____

2. pipo tutunu _____

3. ceket _____

4. kostum _____

5. blucin _____

6. mavi _____

7. dezenfektan _____

8. sunger _____

9. ekmek _____

10. torta _____

CHECK PLEASE!

*Read the true story below, then make an inference
based on the evidence in the story.*

[1]Alfred G. Packer is a famous man in Colorado history. [2]Late in the 19th century, he was convicted of killing and eating Israel Swan, James Humphrey, Frank Miller, Shannon Bell, and George Noon. [3]History has spared us the gruesome details concerning any recipes he may have used in cooking his companions. [4]Despite this blot on his reputation, the University of Colorado, located in Boulder, Colorado, named a building on campus in his honor. [5]What is this building used for?

Your conclusion: _____

Which sentences have the best evidence to support your conclusion? _____   _____

WORD CONNECTIONS

mouth	tight	hound	tip	race
love	rear	state	mine	strain

*Write the word from the choice box that best matches the
meaning of both word sets.   Use each choice box word once.*

1. point   money for service   _____

2. stingy   packed together   _____

3. ancestry   work to the utmost   _____

4. unit of territory   speak   _____

5. running competition division of mankind   _____

6. head opening   where rivers empty   _____

7. to raise   back of something   _____

8. belonging to me   tunnel for ore   _____

9. strong affection   zero points in tennis   _____

10. dog breed   nag   _____

JUST WHAT THE DOCTOR ORDERED

*Read the true story below, then make an inference
based on the evidence in the story.*

[1]Charles Alderson invented a popular soft drink. [2]At the time he was concocting his soft drink, he was dating the lovely daughter of the local physician. [3]Hoping to impress her, he decided to name the drink in honor of her father. [4]What was this girl's last name and what was the name of this soft drink?

Your conclusion: _____

Which sentences have the best evidence to support your conclusion? _____ _____

SPEAKING HUNGARIAN

doll	scotch tape	silk	pills	zero
ambulance	father	deodorant	chewing gum	notebook

*Write the English words from the choice box that best match
the Hungarian words below. Some Hungarian words are
spelled incorrectly to make them easier to pronounce.*

1. notezt _____

2. celluxot _____

3. pagogumi _____

4. dezodoraloszer _____

5. baba _____

6. tablettakat _____

7. mentoautot _____

8. nulla _____

9. apa _____

10. selyem _____

BENNY WAS ALWAYS 39 YEARS OLD

Read the true story below, then make an inference
based on the evidence in the story.

[1]Jack Benny was a much-loved radio, television, and movie star. [2]On his radio and television shows he played a stingy, vain man. [3]One of the most famous of his running gags was that he claimed to be 39 years old. [4]Jack Benny maintained this fiction that he was only 39 years old right up to his death at his real age of 80. [5]Jack Benny's hometown was Waukegan, Illinois, and the town named a city school in his honor. [6]When the school was looking for a nickname for their sports teams, they chose a name that was almost identical to that of a professional football team. [7]By what almost professional-sounding nickname do the school teams call themselves?

Your conclusion: _____

Which sentences have the best evidence to support your conclusion? _____ _____

FIGURE OUT THE ORDER

The story below concerns five crows sitting in a tree who flew away
at different times. Your assignment is to read the story and figure out
which crow flew away first, second, third, and so on. Below the story
is a chart that lists all the possibilities. Use the clues in the story to
cross out possibilities under each crow until you know the answer.

AS THE CROW FLIES

Hecky, Jecky, Wacky, Becky, and Lucky were five crows sitting in a tree. They flew away one at a time so one was first to fly away, another was second, and so on. Hecky, Jecky, and Wacky didn't fly away either first or second. Lucky left after Becky, Wacky left before Hecky, and Jecky left before Wacky.

HECKY	JECKY	WACKY	BECKY	LUCKY
1ST	1ST	1ST	1ST	1ST
2ND	2ND	2ND	2ND	2ND
3RD	3RD	3RD	3RD	3RD
4TH	4TH	4TH	4TH	4TH
5TH	5TH	5TH	5TH	5TH

1st _____ 2nd _____ 3rd _____ 4th _____ 5th _____

JUMPING IN THE SUN

Read the true story below, then make an inference
based on the evidence in the story.

[1]The Mexican jumping bean is really a seed from a shrub found mainly in Mexico. [2]The movement of the seed is actually caused by a caterpillar that has burrowed into the seed and is living there. [3]The seed jumps when the caterpillar inside jerks its body. [4]But the caterpillar apparently knows what it is doing because the unexpected jumping serves an important purpose. [5]Can you deduce this purpose?

Your conclusion: _____

Which sentence has the best evidence to support your conclusion? _____

SPEAKING SWAHILI

goalie	beauty parlor	camera	cake	hotel
bicycle	butcher	father	fine	movie

Write the English words from the choice box that best
match the Swahili words below. Some Swahili words are
spelled incorrectly to make them easier to pronounce.

1. saloni   _____

2. baisikeli   _____

3. bucha   _____

4. keki   _____

5. kemra   _____

6. baba   _____

7. filamu   _____

8. faini   _____

9. gesti   _____

10. kipa   _____

DOING A SERVICE

Read the true story below, then make an inference
based on the evidence in the story.

[1]Sertoma International is an organization of clubs found in Canada, Mexico, Puerto Rico, and the United States. [2]The organization has over 800 clubs and more than 30,000 members. [3]Sertoma clubs provide scholarships, aid orphanages and other worthy institutions, provide services to the handicapped, and sponsor community service projects. [4]The name "Sertoma" derives its name from a three-word description of what the clubs do. [5]What are those three words?

Your conclusion: _____

Which sentences have the best evidence to support your conclusion? _____ _____

SPEAKING CZECH

new	lawyer	baby pacifier	lime	jewelry
husband	salt	tuna	boot	many

Write the English words from the choice box that best
match the Czech words below. Some Czech words are
spelled incorrectly to make them easier to pronounce.

1. tunak   _____

2. novy   _____

3. bota   _____

4. dudlik   _____

5. limeta   _____

6. mnohy   _____

7. advokat   _____

8. sool   _____

9. manzel   _____

10. sperky   _____

DOES THAT BIRD TAKE SHORTHAND?

*Read the true story below, then make an inference
based on the evidence in the story.*

[1]Some names of things made sense at the time they were named but today don't seem to make any sense at all. [2]Such is the case with a large African bird that has tufts of feathers that stick out from its ears. [3]The bird got its name many years ago when people still wrote with quill pens. [4]A quill is a large feather with a clipped end that holds some ink and is a crude sort of fountain pen. [5]In those long-ago days, office workers used quill pens and, when not writing with them, carried their quill pens behind their ears. [6]Anyone going into an office in those long-ago days was used to seeing office employees who appeared to have feathers growing out of their ears. [7]What common name did they give to this African bird?

Your conclusion: _____

Which sentences have the best evidence to support your conclusion? _____ _____

SPEAKING TURKISH

ham	octopus	menu		snack bar	chocolate
sugar	canned food		squid	steak	potato chips

*Write the English words from the choice box that best
match the Turkish words below. Some Turkish words are
spelled incorrectly to make them easier to pronounce.*

1. cikolatah   _____

2. seker   _____

3. konserve   _____

4. cips   _____

5. jambon   _____

6. biftek   _____

7. ahtapod   _____

8. kalamar   _____

9. bufe   _____

10. monuyu   _____

HANGING AROUND WITH THE BIRDS

*Read the true story below, then make an inference
based on the evidence in the story.*

[1]Most birds in the world sleep in the upright position whether they are standing up or sitting down when they sleep. [2]However, there is a parakeet found only in Southeast Asia that sleeps hanging upside down from tree branches at night. [3]Since there aren't that many other creatures that sleep hanging upside down, you should be able to deduce the common name given to this peculiar parakeet. [4]What is that name?

Your conclusion: _____

Which sentence has the best evidence to support your conclusion? _____

SPEAKING RUSSIAN

credit cards	bread	pie	cigar	noodles
apricots	sugar	cough	toothpaste	coffee

*Write the English words from the choice box that best
match the Russian words below. Some Russian words are
spelled incorrectly to make them easier to pronounce.*

1. sigaru   _____

2. zubnaya pasta   _____

3. kashlya   _____

4. kriditny kartachki _____

5. khlyep   _____

6. pirok   _____

7. kofe   _____

8. sakhar   _____

9. makarohy   _____

10. abrikosaf   _____

THOSE ROMANTIC BIRDS

*Read the true story below, then make an inference
based on the evidence in the story.*

[1]Geoffrey Chaucer is considered the greatest English poet of the Middle Ages. [2]He is probably best known for his collection of stories entitled, "The Canterbury Tales." [3]But Chaucer was also something of a naturalist who enjoyed studying bird behavior. [4]This bird study led to the creation of a special day that we still celebrate today. [5]Chaucer observed that on or about one day in the year, birds began to pair off in preparation for nesting. [6]What day would that be?

Your conclusion: _____

Which sentence has the best evidence to support your conclusion? _____

SPEAKING HUNGARIAN

steel	spinach	tourist	coffee	writing tablet
toothpaste	carbonated drink	steak	teacher	taillight

*Write the English words from the choice box that best match
the Hungarian words below. Some Hungarian words are
spelled incorrectly to make them easier to pronounce.*

1. bifsztek   _____

2. acel   _____

3. spenot   _____

4. szoda   _____

5. hatso lampa _____

6. tanito   _____

7. fogkrem   _____

8. turista   _____

9. iropapir   _____

10. kave   _____

ANSWERS

Note: The sentence evidence answers are based on the conclusions listed.

Page 1   7 Up. Other popular theories are that the original bottle held 7 ounces or that there were 7 ingredients in 7 Up.

Best evidence sentence(s): 4

1. arms
2. down
3. duck
4. fling
5. hard
6. join
7. line
8. master
9. mess
10. nag

Page 2 Velcro

Best evidence sentence(s): 5

1. cigarettes
2. speed
3. ballpoint
4. T-shirt
5. teacher
6. toilet paper
7. raincoat
8. jacket
9. butter
10. chocolate

Page 3   Finis is his official name but any variation such as Finish, Finished, or Final are pretty good conclusions.

Best evidence sentence(s): 2, 5

1. tension   The beginning of the words are numbers 2, 4, 6, 8, 10.
2. dukedom   Royal titles are found in the words: queen, count, king, earl, duke.
3. plexus   All the words have names of cars in them: Ford, Dodge, Geo, Saturn, Lexus.

Page 4   Barbara. He named barbiturates after her. Other sources maintain Bayer got the name because he made the discovery on St. Barbara's Day. The name connection of "Barbara" remains the same.

Best evidence sentence(s): 4

1. nice mice
2. fat cat
3. ship trip
4. lucky ducky
5. legal beagle
6. fickle pickle
7. intact pact
8. fuse muse
9. birth mirth
10. dune tune

Page 5 He added tacos to the menu. Glen Bell created the Taco Bell chain of restaurants.

Best evidence sentence(s): 4

1.	ghosts	6.	library
2.	team	7.	short time
3.	train	8.	campground
4.	water	9.	grow plants
5.	teenagers	10.	toothpaste

Page 6 Lincoln visited Monroe, Maryland.

Best evidence sentence(s): 5, 6

1st Ginny, 2nd George, 3rd Greg, 4th Gail

EXPLANATION: The tallest girl picked up the potato first so George and Greg are crossed off under FIRST. The second person to touch the potato was the tallest person in the group and Ginny and Gail are shorter than Greg so Ginny and Gail are crossed off under SECOND. And the second person tossed the potato to a close relative and since Ginny and Gail aren't related you cross off Ginny and Gail under THIRD. Since George and Greg must now be either SECOND and THIRD, they can't be FOURTH so cross off their names under FOURTH. Since Ginny is taller than Gail we now know that Gail wasn't FIRST so cross off her name under FIRST leaving Ginny as the answer and cross off Ginny's name under FOURTH as the only possibility leaving Gail as the answer under FOURTH. Since Greg is the shortest child in his family he couldn't be the tallest in the group so cross off his name under SECOND.

Page 7
Compass plant (*Silphium laciniatum*)

Best evidence sentence(s): 2

1.	automobile	6.	lemonade
2.	diabetic	7.	pig
3.	backbone	8.	milk
4.	sauce	9.	chocolate
5.	fruit	10.	lightbulb

Page 8 Ken and Barbie. Mrs. Handler created the Barbie dolls.

Best evidence sentence(s): 5, 6

1.	yellow	The last letter of the word above begins the next word.
2.	peep	All the words are palindromes.
3.	ungrateful	After the "un" the next letter follows in alphabetical order: c, d, e, f, g.

Page 9 Dickson is credited with inventing the first stick-on bandages.

Best evidence sentence(s): 4

1. soil toil	6. dog's togs
2. mouse louse	7. brain pain
3. sweet beet	8. Bill's pills
4. letter getter	9. groggy froggy
5. twin grin	10. horse course

Page 10 In English the name would be Mount Soap although in Italian the name would be Mount Sapo. Over many centuries the primary ingredients in soap have been animal fat and ashes.

Best evidence sentence(s): 4, 5

1. I'm sorry	6. hour
2. OK	7. round trip
3. United States	8. holidays
4. bank	9. exit
5. coins	10. rearview mirror

Page 11 Californium and Berkelium

Best evidence sentence(s): 1, 3

1. teach	6. trees
2. bake	7. slash
3. glare	8. grow
4. dried	9. clap
5. mopped	10. dance

Page 12 His name was originally John Phillip So and he added the USA to his name to demonstrate his love of this country according to some published accounts.

Best evidence sentence(s): 3

1. gullible	Words with birds in them: owl, hawk, crew, raven, gull.
2. determine	Words with small furry animals in them: hare, rat, sable, mole, ermine.
3. football	Words with two double letters: oo/ii, ee/oo, ee/ss, tt/oo, oo/ll.

Page 13 Cambridge is located on the Cam River. Place names often took their names from local features; in this case, the location of a bridge over the river Cam.

Best evidence sentence(s): 2

1. office gossip
2. farmer
3. training wheels
4. bobby pins
5. garbage can

6. drawer
7. backscrubber
8. toilet tissue
9. bar of soap
10. oven timer

Page 14 Candlefish. Early pioneers noted the Indians using the fish the same way they used candles.

Best evidence sentence(s): 2

1. dingo lingo
2. sub grub
3. doom gloom
4. press dress
5. blaze haze

6. limber timber
7. best vest
8. fowl towel
9. damp tramp
10. trial file

Page 15 "Macedoine de fruits" or fruit salad. Any kind of salad would be basically correct, also a multiple-ingredient such as a stew or goulash.

Best evidence sentence(s): 1, 3

1st Mickey, 2nd Minnie, 3rd Felix, 4th Mopey

EXPLANATION: If Minnie was faster than two others but not the fastest then Minnie was in SECOND place and Mickey, Mopey, and Felix are crossed off under SECOND. (Minnie is crossed off under the other remaining three.) Felix was scratched in the back by another mouse so Felix wasn't last in line and Felix is crossed off under FOURTH. Mickey had a mouse running behind him so he was not FOURTH and his name is crossed off under FOURTH. This leaves Mopey as the answer for FOURTH and Mopey should be crossed off under FIRST and THIRD. Felix is slower than Minnie so Felix must be THIRD and Mickey is crossed off under THIRD. Cross off Felix under FIRST and the puzzle is solved.

Page 16 The famous masterpiece was hung upside down for 47 days before anyone noticed.

Best evidence sentence(s): 2, 4

1. coffee
2. telephone
3. city
4. dolphin
5. to enter

6. kind
7. law
8. accident
9. raincoat
10. English

Page 17 The Tom Thumb Golf Course was, by some published accounts, the first miniature golf course in the United States.

Best evidence sentence(s): 1, 2

1. spun   The vowels are in a, e, i, o, and u order.
2. effete   Words with 3 letters the same in a,b,c,d,and e order.
3. softball   All are balls that are hit rather than thrown or kicked.

Page 18 When an overwhelming favorite loses it is an upset, and "Upset" is the name of the only horse ever to beat Man O'War.

Best evidence sentence(s): 8

1. hand   6. fall
2. general   7. fair
3. form   8. cross
4. fork   9. contract
5. fire   10. cold

Page 19 To hide their hand signals from the opposition, the Gallaudet team was the first to form a huddle before each play.

Best evidence sentence(s): 4, 5

1. to steal   6. aunt
2. father   7. telescope
3. below   8. to drink
4. price   9. above
5. sun   10. milk

Page 20 The "Steagles" were only in existence for one year but true fans of professional football history will never forget them.

Best evidence sentence(s): 3

1st Wallace, 2nd William, 3rd Walter, 4th Wilbur

EXPLANATION: Wallace was allergic to strawberry so Wallace is crossed off under THIRD and FOURTH and Wallace ate his ice cream by licking it so he is crossed off under SECOND. Wallace must have been FIRST in line. Walter ordered after William but wasn't last in line so cross off Walter under FOURTH and William under FOURTH. The only possibility remaining under FOURTH is Wilbur. Since Walter ordered after William he must be THIRD and William must be SECOND.

Page 21 The clever title of the book was "Fowl Tips."

Best evidence sentence(s): 1, 4

1. pack
2. pass
3. produce
4. second
5. tank

6. utter
7. use
8. trip
9. toll
10. press

Page 22 George Washington Whistler invented the train whistle. Oddly enough, he was the father of the famous American artist James McNeill Whistler, and married to "Whistler's Mother."

Best evidence sentence(s): 4

1. cheese
2. laundromat
3. football
4. soccer
5. lunch

6. golf
7. concert
8. restaurant
9. lamp
10. helmet

Page 23 The tuba, of course.

Best evidence sentence(s): 2

1. palmistry   Names of trees in the words: pine, oak, fir, elm, palm.
2. fritter   The first 3 letters are days of the week: Mon, Wed, Sun, Sat, Fri)
3. pendulum   The "pen" alternates between beginning and ending in words.

Page 24 Shovel. In combat, soldiers often dig holes from which they fight.

Best evidence sentence(s): 3

1. funny money
2. phone crone
3. loan bone
4. jewel tool
5. ship drip

6. bird curd
7. prime slime
8. flat cat
9. lumber slumber
10. shoe goo

Page 25 The Pastry War

Best evidence sentence(s): 2

1st Marie, 2nd Don, 3rd Jerry, 4th Rikki

EXPLANATION: A woman finished last so Don and Jerry are crossed off under FOURTH. Don didn't win the race so Don is crossed off under FIRST. Don finished in front of Jerry and Rikki so Don is crossed off under THIRD meaning Don had to finish in SECOND place. The only place left for Jerry is under THIRD place. Since Don finished in front of Rikki then Rikki must have finished in FOURTH place. The only place left is Marie in FIRST place.

Page 26 Mr. Berman sued and won the right to keep baseballs hit into the stands.

Best evidence sentence(s): 4

1. addiction
2. fast
3. drugstore
4. luck
5. stomach
6. land
7. vacation
8. dictionary
9. to act
10. public

Page 27 The featherless chickens were always cold and it cost more to heat the hen houses than it did to remove the feathers from regular chickens,

Best evidence sentence(s): 4

1. pig
2. ice
3. raced
4. dock
5. rat
6. feed
7. wept
8. read
9. jump
10. chew

Page 28 George Bird Grinnell founded the National Audubon Society.

Best evidence sentence(s): 1

1. women
2. vacancy
3. elevator
4. name
5. blanket
6. bugs
7. sink
8. campsite
9. token
10. Chinese

Page 29 The magic word is SHAZAM.

Best evidence sentence(s): 2

1. soapsuds   First vowels after "soap" go in a,e,i,o, u order.
2. meteorologic   Words have 2,3,4,5,6 vowels in progression: e,e; e,ep; e,eo,i; e,e,i,i,a; e,e,o,o,o,i.
3. boondoggle   Words have double vowel then double consonant pattern: oo/ll, ee/ss, oo/tt, ee/ss, oo/gg.

Page 30 All nine states make do with using only 4 letters of the alphabet in the spelling of their names.

Best evidence sentence(s): 1, 2

1. matches
2. flashlight
3. pantry
4. preacher
5. clumsy

6. ears
7. spendthrift
8. lazy person
9. wonderful
10. sausages

Page 31 The most calls are made on Mother's Day. The most collect calls are made on Father's Day.

Best evidence sentence(s): 1, 2

1. hand band
2. wet pet
3. hen pen
4. red bed
5. bad lad

6. bash hash
7. night bite
8. sand land
9. drop pop
10. call ball

Page 32 Horses won't climb circular stairways. Modern firemen no longer need to prevent their horses from climbing the stairs and joining them.

Best evidence sentence(s): 6

1st Jeep, 2nd Lincoln, 3rd Dodge, 4th Ford

EXPLANATION: The Ford and the Jeep received damage on only one end so they are crossed off under SECOND and THIRD. The Dodge was struck in the back by the Ford so the Ford had to be in FOURTH place and the Dodge had to be in THIRD place for it to be struck in the back by the Ford. This means the Jeep had to be in FIRST place since it only had damage on one end. The Lincoln had to be in SECOND place as the only place it could be.

Page 33 Frank Epperson patented the popsicle. The lemonade he left out with the spoon sticking out of it froze solid.

Best evidence sentence(s): 4

1. dog
2. young
3. broken
4. housewife
5. foreign

6. better
7. to be sick
8. ice skating
9. serious
10. flood

Page 34 "Nobody knows" repeated 500 times to make the 1,000 words Hearst requested.

Best evidence sentence(s): 4

1. launch	6. rib
2. legend	7. spare
3. light	8. tire
4. order	9. tramp
5. party	10. trail

Page 35 Uncopyrightable is the only 15-letter English word that never repeats a letter.

Best evidence sentence(s): 3

1. radiator	6. eat
2. boat	7. computer
3. bus	8. chewing gum
4. engineer	9. aspirin
5. Australia	10. surfboard

Page 36 "Mr. Morgan, do you take nose in your tea?"

Best evidence sentence(s): 5, 7

1. glib fib	6. dotty potty
2. last blast	7. rug bug
3. meek creek	8. damp camp
4. rabbit habit	9. calm balm
5. glum chum	10. buy try

Page 37 Poisonous snakes. Africa has more poisonous snakes than Italy.

Best evidence sentence(s): 3

1. boxing	6. palace
2. trousers	7. hobbies
3. mother	8. biscuits
4. muscle	9. one hundred
5. horror	10. ugly

Page 38 Ann Cook's baby portrait appeared on the Gerber baby food jars.

Best evidence sentence(s): 3, 4

1.	strain	Words alternate "ai" and then "ia".
2.	Minnesota	List of states that do not border an ocean
3.	mother	All female relatives.

Page 39 A hammer is a "manually powered fastener-driving impact device."

Best evidence sentence(s): 3

Mon. Thelma, Tues. Tom, Wed. Talya, Thurs. Terry

EXPLANATION: Talya and Terry were not absent MONDAY or TUESDAY so they are crossed off under those two days. Tom and Thelma are crossed off under WEDNESDAY and THURSDAY because Talya and Terry must be absent those two days. Tom is crossed off under MONDAY because he was absent later in the week than Thelma so Tom was absent on TUESDAY and Thelma was absent on MONDAY. This means Talya was absent on WEDNESDAY because Tom was absent the day before Talya.

Page 40 The manager cut out all the songs.

Best evidence sentence(s): 3

1. cast
2. beef
3. hatch
4. junk
5. lead
6. long
7. part
8. quiver
9. refuse
10. rent

Page 41 The critic said Reger's music, like his last name, sounded the same forward as well as backward.

Best evidence sentence(s): 3

1. menu
2. bread
3. beer
4. sugar
5. ham
6. wow
7. painting
8. barbershop
9. more
10. four

Page 42 The 32 South Koreans all publicly cut off a finger. The fingers were then carefully gathered up, wrapped in a newspaper, and presented to the Japanese embassy.

Best evidence sentence(s): 4

1. infrequance   All words used "ance" incorrectly.
2. armament   All words have body parts: leg, neck, toes, ear, arm.
3. smother   Words alternate with names for mother and father: mom, papa, mum, dad, mother.

Page 43 Churchill's two upraised fingers were giving the V for victory sign. Beethoven's Fifth begins with what could be read as dot-dot-dot-dash which is Morse code for the letter V.

Best evidence sentence(s): 1, 3

1. ice cream sandwich	6. fired
2. closing time	7. retirement
3. druggist	8. throat
4. turning signal	9. tableware
5. subway	10. picket fence

Page 44 Santa Claus

Best evidence sentence(s): 4

1st Bel, 2nd Bill, 3rd Bev, 4th Bob, 5th Ben

EXPLANATION: Since none of the children left in the order they were introduced you cross off Bill under FIRST, Bob under SECOND, and so on. Bill left after one girl and before one girl so he is crossed off under FIFTH as FIFTH isn't before anyone. Since a boy left the room last we cross off Bev under FIFTH. Since Bel left before Bev we cross off Bev under FIRST. Since Bob left right after Bev we can cross him out under FIRST. And since Bel left before Bev we cross off Bel under FOURTH. Going back to Bill who left before and after a girl we know that Bill left the room SECOND because no girls left FOURTH and FIFTH meaning one girl had to leave FIRST and one girl had to leave THIRD. Since Bel left before Bev we now know that Bel left FIRST and Bev left THIRD. Since Bob left right after Bev we now know that Bob was FOURTH and Ben had to leave FIFTH.

Page 45 Georgia was named for George II, North and South Carolina were named for Charles I, Maryland was named for Henrietta Maria (not Queen Mary), and Virginia and West Virginia were named for Elizabeth I.

Best evidence sentence(s): 2

1. fiction	6. journalist
2. toothbrush	7. taxi
3. coffee	8. ferry
4. hot	9. tire
5. Europe	10. hotel

Page 46 The kings of clubs, diamonds, spades, and hearts.

Best evidence sentence(s): 2, 4

1. buffaloes   Words alternate animals and objects with horns.
2. observer   Middle letters begin and end next word.
3. methodological   All words have six vowels and 8 consonants.

Page 47 The letter "j" was the last letter added to the English alphabet. The clue is the dot above both the letter "i" and the letter "j."

Best evidence sentence(s): 4

1. fly
2. family
3. watch
4. show
5. room
6. gum
7. man
8. state
9. table
10. corn

Page 48 The Frisbee had no military application.

Best evidence sentence(s): 3

1st Terry, 2nd Toula, 3rd Tom, 4th Tina, 5th Ted

EXPLANATION: TERRY and TOULA both ate twice as many pies as someone else and 100 and 50 are the only two numbers that are twice as much. Cross out 25, 15, and 10 under TERRY and TOULA and 100 and 50 under the other three. TOM ate half as many as Toula so TOM must be 25 and Toula must be 50 and this leaves TERRY with 100. We know TOULA's number is five times TED's number so TED must be 10.

Page 49 Pound cake. The main ingredients all weighed one pound.

Best evidence sentence(s): 2

1. to love
2. to give
3. sleeping bag
4. laundry
5. bread
6. thanks
7. sugar
8. toothpaste
9. leather
10. purple

Page 50 Sadly, Horace Greeley died in 1872—shortly after the election.

Best evidence sentence(s): 5

1. irrigate   All the words have the same vowel on either side of the double letters.
2. disappearance   All the words have fruit in them: apple, lime, plum, peach, pear.
3. slipstream   All the words have bodies of water in them: river, bay, sea, pond, stream.

Page 51 Dandelion. The name comes from the French words, "*dent de lion*," meaning lion's tooth.

Best evidence sentence(s): 3

1. shower	6. department store
2. sign	7. shampoo
3. mailbox	8. knife
4. dancing	9. waitress
5. hockey	10. celery

Page 52 A score of 8 is a snowman because it looks like a snowman.

Best evidence sentence(s): 4

1. umbrella	6. streetlight
2. sweater	7. living quarters
3. suspenders	8. roll call
4. junk	9. doll
5. dress	10. stroller

Page 53 Some historians believed early tennis players used a clock and moved the hands to 15, 30, and 40 to indicate scores.

Best evidence sentence(s): 2

1st Al, 2nd Art, 3rd Abe, 4th Alice, 5th Anne

EXPLANATION: Abe had fewer blisters than the two boys and more blisters than the two girls so Abe had to be in THIRD place. Cross out Abe under FIRST and SECOND and under FOURTH and FIFTH and all the other names under THIRD except for Abe. Al had 5 times as many blisters as Alice and Art had only 4 times as many as Alice so Al must be FIRST and Art must be SECOND. Since Al had 10 times more blisters than Anne and only 5 times as many as Alice then Alice must have had more blisters than Anne putting Alice in FOURTH and Anne in FIFTH.

Page 54 "The one nearest the exit."

Best evidence sentence(s): 5

1. letter	6. climb
2. library	7. school
3. pink	8. vote
4. respect	9. green
5. answer	10. shy

Page 55 LGM stands for "Little Green Men."

Best evidence sentence(s): 5

1. king
2. code
3. bow
4. rice
5. pool

6. blue
7. window
8. chicken
9. apple
10. sign

Page 56 Wall Street

Best evidence sentence(s): 3, 5

1. tweezers
2. underwear
3. cereal
4. sausage
5. lightning

6. seaweed
7. butterfly
8. spider
9. church
10. air mail

Page 57 Popeye, and the vegetable was spinach.

Best evidence sentence(s): 2

1st Mildred, 2nd Mazie, 3rd Mary, 4th Marty, 5th Mike

EXPLANATION: MARY and MIKE took twice as long and the numbers for twice as long are 30 and 20 so 20 and 30 are crossed off under the other names and all the numbers not 20 and 30 are crossed off under MIKE and MARY. MARTY took longer than MARY so MARY had to be 20 and MARTY had to be 24 leaving Mike as the only thing left for 30. MAZIE took 5 seconds less than MARY so MAZIE had to be 15 seconds leaving MILDRED as the answer for 10.

Page 58 The three words are work, health, and love.

Best evidence sentence(s): 4

1. died
2. boss
3. flag
4. nonsense
5. rude

6. understand
7. loud noise
8. exhausted
9. quickly
10. rich

Page 59 Hush Puppies. Hush puppies are deep-fried corn bread.

Best evidence sentence(s): 3

1. interrogate   All are "asking" words.
2. rattletrap   All words have names of snakes in them: boa, coral, adder, rattle.
3. generally   All words have military titles: captain, private, admiral, major, general.

Page 60 Ink, Arkansas. The voters took the instructions literally and wrote in "Ink."

Best evidence sentence(s): 5

1. bookstore   6. children
2. office supplies   7. emergency
3. stage show   8. influenza
4. save   9. pill
5. delete   10. pain killer

Page 61 Hanson Gregory is credited with making the first doughnut hole because he
disliked the way his mother's doughnuts had a soggy center.

Best evidence sentence(s): 3

1st Car 12, 2nd Car 37, 3rd Car 54, 4th Car 21, 5th Car 31

EXPLANATION: Car 21 and car 31 are FOURTH and FIFTH place so all the other
numbers are crossed off under those two places and Car 21 and Car 31 are crossed off
under the first THREE places. Car 54 finished behind Car 37 so Car 54 is crossed off
under FIRST place and Car 37 is crossed off under THIRD place. Car 12 must be first
because it finished in FRONT of Car 37 and Car 37 must be SECOND place to finish in
front of Car 54. Car 21 as the fourth-highest number finished in front of the third-highest
number so Car 21 must be FOURTH and Car 31 FIFTH.

Page 62 The ancient custom was cannibalism. Today, there are no tribes still practicing
cannibalism in the Ivory Coast.

Best evidence sentence(s): 4

1. bag   6. model
2. wheel   7. deck
3. box   8. diamond
4. baby   9. down
5. ball   10. fountain

Page 63 Anaximenes requested that Alexander destroy the town. Since Alexander had
vowed not to do what Anaximenes requested, he had no choice but to spare the
town.

Best evidence sentence(s): 7

1. behind
2. alarm clock
3. coat
4. dark
5. dancing

6. false
7. garden
8. hairbrush
9. cuckoo clock
10. raincoat

Page 64 The second invention was the water heater. This invention created a need for a hot water faucet. Since most people are right-handed the cold water tap was mounted to the right leaving the left-hand side for the hot water faucet.

Best evidence sentence(s): 3

1. naked
2. sideways
3. clothespins
4. installment plan
5. tongue

6. risky
7. fingerprints
8. promotion
9. selling
10. killer

Page 65 The whole review read, "Guido Nasso: nazzo guido."

Best evidence sentence(s): 5

1. toothpaste
2. hairbrush
3. great
4. food
5. dangerous

6. cat
7. light
8. ask
9. candle
10. porter

Page 66 Color-blind people. They can tell when a color is lit up but they can't see what color it is. If the traffic lights didn't follow the same pattern they wouldn't know what to do at traffic lights.

Best evidence sentence(s): 3

1st Lena, 2nd Bosco, 3rd Ralph, 4th Tippi, 5th Lance

EXPLANATION: Lance, Tippi, and Ralph are crossed out under FIRST and SECOND and Lena and Bosco are crossed off under THIRD, FOURTH, and FIFTH. Tippi laughed when Ralph fell out of the tree so Tippi wasn't THIRD and there was a monkey in the tree when Tippi fell so Tippi wasn't FIFTH. This only leaves FOURTH place open for Tippi meaning Ralph must be THIRD and Lance must be FIFTH. Bosco was still in the tree when Lena fell so Bosco must be SECOND and Lena FIRST.

Page 67 Round manhole covers can't fall through the hole. Square and rectangular ones can fall though diagonally.

Best evidence sentence(s): 3

1. delay
2. face
3. fight
4. help
5. light
6. occupation
7. scissors
8. song
9. boiled
10. trout

Page 68 Wedding day. The tradition is carrying the bride over the threshold. The thinking was that on her wedding day the bride would be too nervous to walk properly.

Best evidence sentence(s): 4

1. orange
2. lemonade
3. rainy
4. e-mail
5. litter
6. tiger
7. rules
8. picnic
9. visa
10. pump

Page 69 Norway. People from Norway are Norwegians. Shortened to "weejuns" it all makes sense.

Best evidence sentence(s): 3

1. traffic lights
2. sculpture
3. refuse
4. big
5. lightbulb
6. greedy
7. to dance
8. detergent
9. gardens
10. hat

Page 70 Doors to public buildings open outward in case of panic caused by a fire or some other emergency.

Best evidence sentence(s): 4

1. fresh
2. to win
3. to have
4. good
5. cat
6. children
7. comedy
8. kiss
9. style
10. teacher

Page 71 In hot weather they stand head to tail because flicking their tails drives insects away from their heads. In cold weather, they stand head to head because their hot breath helps keep them warm.

Best evidence sentence(s): 3

1. silly billy
2. dull gull
3. foggy doggy
4. shovel hovel
5. fine brine
6. louder chowder
7. lobster mobster
8. mellow fellow
9. grove trove
10. lazy daisy

Page 72 Marion Donovan is credited with inventing the disposable diaper.

Best evidence sentence(s): 3

Bonnie 250, Benny 200, Byron 125, Boris 100, Belle 50

EXPLANATION: BENNY, BONNIE, and BORIS must be 250, 200, and 100 as twice as much and BELLE and BYRON must be 125 and 50. BYRON must be 125 meaning BELLE must be 50 and BORIS must be 100. BYRON ate half as much as BONNIE so BONNIE must be 250 and BENNY must be 200 as the only number left.

Page 73 When arranged correctly, their initials are CABAL.

Best evidence sentence(s): 3

1. bacon
2. drudge
3. scatterbrained
4. excited
5. warehouse
6. renter
7. wind gust
8. dusk
9. two weeks
10. expert

Page 74 Caligua had his soldiers fill the chests with seashells.

Best evidence sentence(s): 1, 6

1. nothing
2. misery
3. quiet
4. good night
5. friend
6. business
7. teacher
8. salary
9. hungry
10. driver

Page 75 Outdoor billboards. The awards are given by the Outdoor Advertising Association of American marketing.

Best evidence sentence(s): 4

1. page
2. poster
3. shower
4. towel
5. size
6. film
7. matches
8. party
9. cabbage
10. lemonade

Page 76 We call it a rainbow.

Best evidence sentence(s): 2, 3

1. asparagus
2. cake
3. lemon
4. city
5. daughter
6. muggy
7. helpful
8. luggage
9. party
10. ship

Page 77 Arby's. The Raffel brothers got the "r" sound from their initial and the "b" from the initial of brothers.

Best evidence sentence(s): 1, 3

1. tooter rooter
2. least beast
3. clean bean
4. cooler jeweler
5. mash trash
6. single tingle
7. rare bear
8. roach coach
9. real meal
10. loaves stoves

Page 78 Eddie Gaedal was a 3 foot, 7-inch midget. The strike zone on him would be so small that he was almost certain to draw a walk every time he came to bat.

Best evidence sentence(s): 3, 6

Tango 75, Bongo 70, Bingo 65, Chico 40, Koko 35

EXPLANATION: BONGO, TANGO, and CHICO had to be numbers 75, 70, or 40 as those three numbers are five more than a number behind them. Cross off 65 and 35 under those three gorillas and cross off 75, 70, and 40 under BINGO and KOKO. BINGO must be 65 and TANGO must be 75 as the only possibility for numbers 10 less. KOKO must be 35 as it is the only number left for him. CHICO must be 40 as he stuffed less than BONGO whose number must be 70.

Page 79 People don't take dead cats to the veterinarian. The veterinarians only saw the survivors and didn't see the majority of cats which died in falls from great heights.

Best evidence sentence(s): 2, 4

1.	far jar	6.	rotten cotton
2.	stone crone	7.	wandering pondering
3.	ample sample	8.	damp lamp
4.	smelly belly	9.	field yield
5.	meal deal	10.	handy candy

Page 80 The entire book was written without using the letter "e" as was the paragraph.

Best evidence sentence(s): 2

1.	soap	6.	command
2.	fire	7.	wet
3.	bonds	8.	one
4.	gum	9.	button
5.	light	10.	rise

Page 81 During the discussion that followed Beatty's speech, the extras decided they weren't being paid enough and went on strike demanding a pay raise. Warren Beatty granted them a pay raise and the filming continued.

Best evidence sentence(s): 3, 4

1.	OK	6.	restaurant
2.	mayonnaise	7.	check
3.	salad	8.	son
4.	wine	9.	television
5.	asthma	10.	custard

Page 82 James Dewar invented the thermos bottle. We still use the basic design he invented in 1892.

Best evidence sentence(s): 4

1.	accelerator	6.	towel
2.	fan	7.	clock
3.	light	8.	terrace
4.	mailbox	9.	vase
5.	bellhop	10.	lemonade

Page 83 The decorative fish is commonly known as the "tilefish."

Best evidence sentence(s): 3

1. suitcase	6. campsite
2. newspaper	7. bus
3. flu	8. movie theater
4. toilet	9. gas station
5. gallery	10. ticket

Page 84 This clever bird is commonly called the "tailorbird."

Best evidence sentence(s): 2

1. lip balm	6. third
2. flu	7. toilet
3. map	8. rackets
4. Greece	9. concert
5. July	10. zoo

Page 85 These flowers are commonly called "day lilies."

Best evidence sentence(s): 3

1. hello	6. diesel
2. seventy	7. battery
3. receipt	8. elevator
4. bus	9. newspaper
5. cabin	10. Internet

Page 86 Animated films. The "Annies" are awarded by the Internationl Animated Film Society.

Best evidence sentence(s): 3

1. ruddy buddy	6. spill Bill
2. straight eight	7. mountain fountain
3. carriage marriage	8. city biddy
4. fix Bics	9. cattle battle
5. desire mire	10. handy candy

Page 87 These birds are commonly known as "turnstone birds."

Best evidence sentence(s): 2

1. water	6. bus
2. weekend	7. Saturday
3. Europe	8. alcohol
4. photograph	9. tennis court
5. milk	10. garage

Page 88 The letter "Q" still has its monkey tail.

Best evidence sentence(s): 1, 3

1. cake shop	6. tea
2. museum	7. water
3. cab	8. heater
4. train	9. lipstick
5. balcony	10. postcard

Page 89 These insects are commonly known as "stinkbugs."

Best evidence sentence(s): 1

1. ticket	6. passport
2. swimming pool	7. air mail
3. airport	8. Canada
4. engine	9. radio
5. hello	10. address

Page 90 The winter and summer Olympic games are no longer held in the same year.

Best evidence sentence(s): 2, 3

1. fresh	6. campsite
2. mayonnaise	7. blouse
3. sugar	8. jacket
4. potato salad	9. pajamas
5. lemon	10. ceramics

Page 91 The six gases were called "noble" because they don't readily mix with other elements. However, it was later discovered that krypton, radon, and xenon will combine with fluorine to form compounds.

Best evidence sentence(s): 3

1. towel	6. apartment
2. golf course	7. Band-Aid
3. week	8. bath
4. ambulance	9. budget
5. America	10. cobra

Page 92 Land's End

Best evidence sentence(s): 2, 3

1. Asia
2. thirty
3. none
4. telephone
5. volleyball

6. coach
7. toilets
8. movies
9. home
10. guitar

Page 93 Goatsucker

Best evidence sentence(s): 2

1. flash bulbs
2. pipe tobacco
3. jacket
4. tailored suit
5. jeans

6. blue color
7. disinfectant
8. sponge
9. bread
10. tart

Page 94 The Alfred Packer Grill is the school's cafeteria. Of course, any answer such as restaurant or snack shop would be acceptable.

Best evidence sentence(s): 2, 3

1. tip
2. tight
3. strain
4. state
5. race

6. mouth
7. rear
8. mine
9. love
10. hound

Page 95 Dr. Pepper was his girlfriend's father.

Best evidence sentence(s): 2, 3

1. notebook
2. scotch tape
3. chewing gum
4. deodorant
5. doll

6. pills
7. ambulance
8. zero
9. father
10. silk

Page 96 The Jack Benny School teams are known as the "39ers."

Best evidence sentence(s): 3, 6

1st Becky, 2nd Lucky, 3rd Jecky, 4th Wacky, 5th Hecky

EXPLANATION: HECKY, JECKY, AND WACKY have 1st and 2nd crossed off and BECKY and LUCKY have 3rd, 4th, and 5th crossed off. LUCKY left after BECKY so BECKY left 1st and LUCKY 2nd. WACKY left before HECKY so WACKY didn't leave 5th. JECKY left before WACKY so WACKY didn't leave 5th. This means HECKY had to leave 5th as the only crow who could have done so. Only 3rd and 4th are still possibilities and since JECKY left before WACKY then JECKY must be 3rd and WACKY must be 4th.

Page 97 Scientists believe the unexpected jumping of the bean scares away birds and animals that might be inclined to eat it.

Best evidence sentence(s): 4

1. beauty parlor
2. bicycle
3. butcher
4. cake
5. camera
6. father
7. movie
8. fine
9. hotel
10. goalie

Page 98 Service to mankind.

Best evidence sentence(s): 3, 4

1. tuna
2. new
3. boot
4. baby pacifier
5. lime
6. many
7. lawyer
8. salt
9. husband
10. jewelry

Page 99 Secretary bird (*Sagittarius serpentarius*). Early African explorers who named the bird thought it reminded them of secretaries back home.

Best evidence sentence(s): 4, 5

1. chocolate
2. sugar
3. canned food
4. potato chips
5. ham
6. steak
7. octopus
8. squid
9. snack bar
10. menu

Page 100 The bat parakeet

Best evidence sentence(s): 2

1. cigar
2. toothpaste
3. cough
4. credit cards
5. bread
6. pie
7. coffee
8. sugar
9. noodles
10. apricots

Page 101 Chaucer noted birds pairing off on February 14th, Valentine's Day.

Best evidence sentence(s): 5

1. steak
2. steel
3. spinach
4. carbonated drink
5. taillight
6. teacher
7. toothpaste
8. tourist
9. writing tablet
10. coffee

Lesson 1

PREFIX	
con-	with, together
de-	from, away, down, apart; not
infra-	beneath
ob-	to, toward, against
re-	back, again

ROOT	
struct	build

SUFFIX	
-ion	an action or process; state, quality, act
-ure	state, quality, act; that which; process, condition

A. Spelling and Defining Words

Write each word from the choice box next to its definition.

destruction	destruct	infrastructure	construct
reconstruct	reconstruction	structure	construction
obstruction	obstruct		

1. _____ to deliberately destroy an object

2. _____ underlying framework of a system

3. _____ the action or process of building

4. _____ the act of destroying; a state of damage

5. _____ to put back together again

6. _____ that which is built in a particular way

7. _____ an obstacle put up against something else

8. _____ the act of putting back together

9. _____ to block or fill with obstacles

10. _____ to form by putting together parts

B. Completing the Sentence
Write the best word from the gray box to complete each sentence.

1. The hurricane that struck the Florida coast caused a great deal of _____.

   reconstruction   destruction   obstruction

2. The accident on the highway was a major _____ to the flow of traffic.

   structure   construction   obstruction

3. Jeremy kept busy all afternoon with the _____ of his Lego® tower from the fallen pieces.

   destruction   reconstruction   construction

4. The _____ of a school consists of teachers, administration, and a school board.

   infrastructure   construction   structure

5. He was hoping to _____ the new model airplane within a week.

   destruct   construct   reconstruct

6. The _____ of the new bridge took two years.

   construction   destruction   obstruction

7. A large _____ is being erected on the old fairground site.

   infrastructure   obstruction   structure

8. If the dead tree should fall it will _____ the road.

   obstruct   construct   destruct

9. In the science fiction movie, the plan was to _____ the space vehicle.

   structure   destruction   destruct

10. In order to solve the case, the detective had to _____ the crime scene.

   reconstruct   structure   obstruct